The Pragmatic theory developed by Peirce, James and Dewey

Denton Loring Geyer

Alpha Editions

This edition published in 2024

ISBN 9789361473944

Design and Setting By

Alpha Editions
www.alphaedis.com

Email - info@alphaedis.com

As per information held with us this book is in Public Domain.
This book is a reproduction of an important historical work.
Alpha Editions uses the best technology to reproduce historical work
in the same manner it was first published to preserve its original nature.
Any marks or number seen are left intentionally to preserve.

Contents

INTRODUCTORY.	- 1 -
CHAPTER I. THE PRAGMATIC DOCTRINE AS ORIGINALLY PROPOSED BY PEIRCE.	- 3 -
CHAPTER II. The Interpretation Given to Pragmatism by James.	- 16 -
JAMES' EXPOSITION OF PEIRCE.	- 16 -
DEVELOPMENT OF THE DOCTRINE THROUGH THE EARLIER WRITINGS OF JAMES.	- 19 -
THE THEORY OF TRUTH IN 'PRAGMATISM' AND 'THE MEANING OF TRUTH'.	- 25 -
CHAPTER III. The Pragmatic Doctrine as Set Forth by Dewey.	- 35 -
CONTRAST BETWEEN JAMES AND DEWEY.	- 38 -
CHAPTER IV. Summary and Conclusion.	- 42 -
Footnotes	- 45 -
BIBLIOGRAPHY	- 47 -
THE WORKS OF CHARLES SANDERS PEIRCE	- 47 -
THE WORKS OF WILLIAM JAMES	- 49 -
THE WORKS OF JOHN DEWEY	- 49 -
WORKS ON TRUTH	- 56 -
WORKS ON PRAGMATISM	- 63 -
VITA.	- 77 -

INTRODUCTORY.

This thesis attempts to trace the growth of the pragmatic doctrine of truth through the works of its three most famous advocates in America.

An examination of Peirce's initial statement of pragmatism is followed by a discussion of his objections to the meaning put upon his doctrine by his would-be disciples, and his resort, in order to save himself from these 'perversions', to a renaming of his theory. Some evident contradictions in his different principles are pointed out.

The changing position of William James is then followed through magazine articles and books appearing successively during a period of about thirty years. One finds here a gradually but continually widening divergence from the rationalistic theories, which culminates finally in the much-quoted extreme statements of the book 'Pragmatism'. The few subsequently published references to truth seem to consist largely of defenses or retractions of the tenets there set forth. As has been so often said, William James was too sympathetic toward the doctrines of other men to maintain a consistent doctrine of his own. His best work, like that of the higher literary type to which he approached, was to transcribe and interpret the feelings of other men. His genius lay in the clearness with which he could translate these ideas and the lucid fashion in which he could cut to the heart of ambiguities in them. With the highest and most sincere admiration for the spirit of James' labors in philosophy and psychology, the writer is unable to find there permanent contributions to the solution of the particular problem which we have before us here, the problem of truth. In his splendid protest against all static theories, he seems to have accepted pragmatism for what it was not rather than for what it was. It was not a cut-and-dried system leaving no room for individuality, and that this was one of his strongest reasons for accepting it is shown by his asking again and again: "If this (pragmatism) is not truth, what is?" He was attempting to find a theory—almost any theory, one thinks sometimes—which would serve as an alternative to the older doctrines so incompatible with his temperament.

It is interesting to note that the frequent protests made by Peirce against the turn given his ideas by his followers are always directed against the work of James and Schiller, and never, so far as I have been able to ascertain, against that of Dewey. It therefore seems worth while to undertake a direct comparison between the views of Peirce and Dewey. This comparison, then, occupies the latter part of the thesis, with the result, it may be said at once, that Dewey's work is found to be very closely related to the original formulation of pragmatism as made by Peirce.

The excellent historical sketches of pragmatism which have appeared during the last five years1 have been somewhat broader in scope than the present treatise, for they have usually described the development of all the pragmatic doctrines in the mass while the emphasis here is placed on the intensive treatment of a single doctrine, and this doctrine is followed, moreover, through a limited number of its expounders. Further, almost all such sketches are taken up for the most part in showing how pragmatism grew out of the older doctrines or in contrasting it with various alternative theories while the thing attempted here is, again, a careful comparison of the views of three thinkers within the School itself—with of course the writer's own reaction to these views. It has thus seemed best to undertake no (necessarily fragmentary) treatment of truth as 'intuition' or 'coherence' or 'correspondence' or the rest.

General criticism of the pragmatic theory of truth, as is evident to anyone who has followed the controversy, has been principally directed against the more 'radical' statements of James and Schiller. Whether this is merely because these champions of the theory are more extreme, or whether they are really more prone to errors in their reasoning, we need not determine here. But it is worth pointing out that, on the other hand, if Peirce and Dewey were to be taken as the truer representatives of pragmatism a large part of the flood of recent criticism would be irrelevant. This is by no means to say that the work of Peirce and Dewey is above criticism; it is merely to call attention to the fact that most of the criticism of pragmatism is directed against principles which these two men do not happen to hold. An understanding of the doctrine in its more conservative terms, however, is certainly on the increase, and we are seldom nowadays burdened with refutations of such alleged pragmatism as that anything is true which it is pleasant to believe or that any theory of procedure is true which happens to turn out well.

CHAPTER I.
THE PRAGMATIC DOCTRINE AS ORIGINALLY PROPOSED BY PEIRCE.

Pragmatism has been described as an attitude of mind, as a method of investigation, and as a theory of truth. The attitude is that of looking forward to outcomes rather than back to origins. The method is the use of actual or possible outcomes of our ideas to determine these ideas' real meaning. The theory of truth defines the truth of our beliefs in terms of the outcome of these beliefs.

Pragmatism as a principle of method, like the Mendelian laws of heredity, lay for decades in oblivion. It was brought to light and to the world's notice in 1898 by William James, who by his wonderful literary style immediately gave it the widest currency. The doctrine was originally proposed in 1878 by C. S. Peirce in a paper for the Popular Science Monthly entitled "How To Make Our Ideas Clear." This article was the second of six on the general topic. "Illustrations of the Logic of Science." The other articles of the series were respectively called "The Fixation of Belief," "The Doctrine of Chances," "The Probability of Induction," "The Order of Nature," and "Induction, Deduction, and Hypothesis."

In the famous discussion of How To Make Our Ideas Clear, Peirce pointed out that by a *clear* idea is meant, according to the logicians, one which will be recognized wherever it is met with, so that no other will be mistaken for it. But since to do this without exception is impossible to human beings, and since to have such acquaintance with the idea as to have lost all hesitancy in recognizing it *in ordinary cases* amounts only to a subjective feeling of mastery which may be entirely mistaken, they supplement the idea of 'clearness' with that of 'distinctness'. A distinct idea is defined as one that contains nothing which is not clear. By the *contents* of an idea logicians understand whatever is contained in its definition, so that an idea is *distinctly* apprehended, according to them, when we can give a precise definition of it, in abstract terms. Here the professional logicians leave the subject, but it is easy to show that the doctrine that familiar use and abstract distinctness make the perfection of apprehension, "has its only true place in philosophies which have long been extinct", and it is now time to formulate a method of attaining "a more perfect clearness of thought such as we see and admire in the thinkers of our own time".

The action of thought is excited by the irritation of a doubt, and ceases when belief is attained; so that the production of belief is the sole function of thought. As thought appeases the irritation of a doubt, which is the motive for thinking, it relaxes and comes to rest for a moment when belief is reached. But belief is a rule for action, and its application requires further thought and further doubt, so that at the same time that it is a stopping place it is also a new starting place for thought. The final upshot of thinking is the exercise of volition.

"The essence of belief is the establishment of a habit, and different beliefs are distinguished by the different modes of action to which they give rise. If beliefs do not differ in this respect, if they appease the same doubt by producing the same rule of action, then no more differences in the manner of consciousness of them can make them different beliefs, any more than playing a tune in different keys is playing a different tune."

Imaginary distinctions are made very frequently, it is true, between beliefs which differ only in their mode of expression. Such false distinctions do as much harm as the confusion of beliefs really different. "One singular deception of this sort, which often occurs, is to mistake the sensation produced by our own unclearness of thought for a character of the object we are thinking. Instead of perceiving that the obscurity is purely subjective, we fancy that we contemplate a quality of the object which is essentially mysterious; and if our conception be afterwards presented to us in a clear form we do not recognize it as the same, owing to the absence of the feeling of unintelligibility.... Another such deception is to mistake a mere difference in the grammatical construction of two words for a distinction between the ideas they express.... From all these sophisms we shall be perfectly safe so long as we reflect that the whole function of thought is to produce habits of action; and that whatever is connected with a thought, but irrelevant to its purpose, is an accretion to it, but no part of it".

"To develop a meaning we have, therefore, simply to determine what habits it produces, for what a thing means is simply what habits it involves. Now the identity of a habit depends on how it might lead us to act, not merely under such circumstances as are likely to arise, but under such as might possibly occur, no matter how improbable.... Thus we come down to what is tangible and practical as the root of every real distinction of thought, no matter how *subtle* it may be; and there is no distinction so fine as to consist in anything but a possible difference in practice".

As an example, consider the doctrine of transubstantiation. Are the elements of the sacrament flesh and blood 'only in a tropical sense' or are they literally just that? Now "we have no conception of wine except what may enter into a belief either, (1) that this, that, or the other is wine, or (2) that wine possesses certain properties. Such beliefs are nothing but self-notifications that we should, upon occasion, act in regard to such things as we believe to be wine according to the qualities which we believe wine to possess. The occasion of such action would be some sensible perception, the motive of it to produce some sensible result. Thus our action has exclusive reference to what affects our senses, our habit has the same bearing as our action, our belief the same as our habit, our conception the same as our belief; and we can consequently mean nothing by wine but what has certain effects, direct or indirect, upon the senses; and to talk of something as having all the sensible characters of wine, yet being in reality blood, is senseless jargon.... Our idea of anything *is* our idea of its sensible effects; and if we fancy that we have any other, we deceive ourselves, and mistake a mere sensation accompanying the thought for a part of the thought itself".

"It appears, then, that the rule for attaining ... clearness of apprehension is as follows: *Consider what effects, which might conceivably have practical bearings, we conceive the object of our conception to have. Then, our conception of these effects is the whole of our conception of the object*". (Italics mine).

An application of this method to a conception which particularly concerns logic occupies the last section of the article,—a use of the method to make clear our conception of "reality". Considering clearness in the sense of familiarity, no idea could be clearer than this, for everyone uses it with perfect confidence. Clearness in the sense of definition is only slightly more difficult,—"we may define the real as that whose characters are independent of what anybody may think them to be". But however satisfactory this is as a definition, it does not by any means make our idea of reality perfectly clear. "Here, then, let us apply our rules. According to them, reality, like every other quality, consists in the peculiar sensible effects which things partaking of it produce. The only effect which real things have is to cause belief, for all the sensations which they excite emerge into consciousness in the form of beliefs. The question therefore is, how is true belief (or belief in the real) distinguished from false belief (belief in fiction)". Briefly this may be answered by saying that the true belief is the one which will be arrived at after a complete examination of all the evidence. "That opinion which is fated to be ultimately agreed to by all who investigate, is what we mean by the truth, and the object represented in this opinion is the real." (Note: "Fate means merely that which is sure to come true, and can nohow be avoided".) The real thus depends indeed upon what is ultimately thought about it, but not upon what any particular person thinks about it. This is clearly brought out in contrast to non-scientific investigation, where personal equation counts for a great deal more. "It is hard to convince a follower of the *a priori* method by adducing facts; but show him that an opinion that he is defending is inconsistent with what he has laid down elsewhere, and he will be very apt to retract it. These minds do not seem to believe that disputation is ever to cease; they seem to think that the opinion which is natural for one man is not so for another, and that belief will, consequently, never be settled. In contenting themselves with fixing their own opinions by a method which would lead another man to a different result, they betray their feeble hold upon the conception of what truth is. On the other hand, all the followers of science are fully persuaded that the processes of investigation, if only pushed far enough, will give one certain solution to every question to which they can be applied. One man may investigate the velocity of light by studying the transits of Venus and the aberration of the stars; another by the opposition of Mars and eclipses of Jupiter's satellites; a third by the method of Fizian.... They may at first obtain different results, but as each perfects his method and his processes, the results will move steadily together toward a destined center. So with all scientific research. Different minds may set out with the most antagonistic views, but the process of investigation carries them by a force outside of themselves to one and the same conclusion". This conclusion, to be sure, may be long postponed, and might indeed be preceded by a false belief which should be accepted universally. But "the opinion which would finally result from investigation does not depend on how anybody may actually think.... The reality of that which is real does depend on the real fact that the investigation is destined to lead, at last, if continued long enough, to a belief in it".

It will be seen that this article does not intend to put forward any new theory of truth. It is simply an attempt at expounding a new theory of clearness. Peirce desires to describe a new way of clearing up metaphysical disputes, the method, namely, of finding the meaning of each question by reducing it to its experimental consequences.

For Peirce a doctrine could be perfectly clear and yet false. This would be the case where one had a vivid idea of all the outcomes in experience involved by the idea, but yet was unable to prophesy any outcome that should be verified by future fact. Our idea of the object would not in that case 'correspond to the reality' in the sense of giving us a belief which could be 'verified by all investigators'.

Peirce, then, instead of having a radical and startling theory of truth to propose, would consider himself an ultra-conservative on the question of what shall be called truth. Approaching the matter from the standpoint of a scientist, (for he says in another connection that he had at this time spent most of his life in a laboratory), he is concerned only with an attempt to apply "the fruitful methods of science" to "the barren field of metaphysics". For metaphysics seems to him very much in need of outside help. His different conception of the two disciplines may be seen from the following passage. In contrast to philosophy, he is eulogizing the natural sciences, "where investigators, instead of condemning each the work of the others as misdirected from beginning to end, co-operate, stand upon one another's shoulders, and multiply incontestable results; where every observation is repeated, and isolated observations count for little; where every hypothesis that merits attention is subjected to severe but fair examination, and only after the predictions to which it leads have been remarkably borne out by experience is trusted at all, and then only provisionally; where a radically false step is rarely taken, even the most faulty of those theories which gain credence being true in their main experiential predictions".

It is in a desire to elevate metaphysics to somewhere near this level that Peirce proposes his new theory of clearness, believing that much of the useless disputation of philosophy, as he sees it, will end when we know exactly what we are talking about according to this test.

On the question of truth he might indeed have referred to another of his early articles, where the same idea of the independence of truth from individual opinion is brought out. The much-quoted paper on "How To Make Our Ideas Clear" was, as we have noted, the second of a series called "Illustrations of the Logic of Science". In order to get his doctrine of truth more adequately before us, we may turn for a moment to the first article of the series, the paper called "The Fixation of Belief".

Here Peirce begins by pointing out four methods for fixing belief. In the first, or 'method of tenacity', one simply picks out the belief which for some reason he *desires*, and holds to it by closing his eyes to all evidence pointing the other way. The second, or the 'method of authority', is the same except that the individual is replaced by the state. The third, or 'a priori method', makes a thing true when it is 'agreeable to reason'. But this sort of truth varies between persons, for what is agreeable to reason is more or less a matter of taste.

In contrast with these, and especially with the *a priori* method, a method must be discovered which will determine truth entirely apart from individual opinion. This is the method of science. That is, "To satisfy our doubt ... it is necessary that a method should be found by which our beliefs may be caused by nothing human, but by some external permanency—by something upon which our thinking has no effect.... It must be something which affects, or might affect, every man. And, though these affections are necessarily as various as are individual conditions, yet the method must be such that the ultimate conclusion of every man shall be the same. Such is the method of science. Its fundamental hypothesis, restated in more familiar language, is this: There are real things whose characters are entirely independent of our opinions about them; those realities affect our senses according to regular laws, and, though our sensations are as different as our relations to the objects, yet, by taking advantage of the laws of perception, we can ascertain by reasoning how things really are, and any man, if he have sufficient experience, and reason enough about it, will be led to one true conclusion. The new conception here involved is that of reality. It may be asked how I know that there are any realities. If this hypothesis is the sole support of my method of inquiry, my method of inquiry must not be used to support my hypothesis. The reply is this: 1. If investigation cannot be regarded as proving that there are real things, it at least does not lead to a contrary conclusion; but the method and conception on which it is based remain ever in harmony. No doubts of the method, therefore, arise with its practice, as is the case with all the others. 2. The feeling which gives rise to any method of fixing belief is a dissatisfaction at two repugnant propositions. But here already is a vague concession that there is some *one* thing to which a proposition should conform.... Nobody, therefore, can really doubt that there are realities, or, if he did, doubt would not be a source of dissatisfaction. The hypothesis, therefore, is one which every mind admits. So that the social impulse does not cause me to doubt it. 3. Everybody uses the scientific method about a great many things, and only ceases to use it when he does not know how to apply it. 4. Experience of the method has not led me to doubt it, but, on the contrary, scientific investigation has had the most wonderful triumphs in the way of settling opinion. These afford the explanation of my not doubting the method or the hypothesis which it supposes". (p.12)

The method of science, therefore, is procedure based on the hypothesis that there are realities independent of what we may think them to be. This, it seems, is what Peirce regards as the fundamental principle of the 'logic of science'. This principle, stated here in the first paper, is again stated as we have seen, towards the close of the second paper. There he says again, "All the followers of science are fully persuaded that the processes of investigation, if only pushed far enough, will give one certain solution to every question to which they can be applied.... Different minds may set out with the most antagonistic views, but the progress of investigation carries them by a force outside of themselves to one and the same conclusion.... This great law is embodied in the conception of truth and reality. That opinion which is fated to be ultimately agreed to by all who investigate, is what we mean by truth, and the object represented in this opinion is the real. This is the way I would explain reality". (p.300).

It is well at this point to call attention to a distinction. It is to be noticed that in the first paper and in the latter part of the second he is talking of a method for attaining truth. But in the body of the second paper he is talking of a method for attaining clearness. These two should be kept distinct in our minds. The use of the various methods described for finding the velocity of light were endeavors to find the truth, not to make our ideas clear. Clearness and truth Peirce believes to have no invariable connection. He says in ending the article on "How To Make Our Ideas Clear", "It is certainly important to know how to make our ideas clear, *but they may be ever so clear without being true*". (p.302, italics mine.) There are, then, two methods under consideration: the scientific method for reaching truth, with its postulate that there are independent realities, and the logical method for securing clearness, which as he has just stated, has no necessary connection with truth.

Now I should like to point out, in criticism, that these two methods cannot be used together, or rather that the postulate of the 'scientific method' will not endure the test proposed by the 'method for clearness'. The scientific method postulates a reality unaffected by our opinions about it. But when we apply the method for clearness to this reality it seems to vanish.

The process is this: Peirce, as we will remember, begins his discussion of the real by defining it as "that whose characters are independent of what anybody may think them to be." Then passing on to apply his method for clearness he finds that "reality, like every other quality, consists in the peculiar sensible effects which things partaking of it produce", and adds that "the only effects which real things have is to cause belief, for all the sensations which they excite emerge into consciousness in the form of beliefs". Reality is the sum of its sensible effects, its sensible effects are beliefs, so reality is a sum of beliefs.

Now, reality cannot be the sum of *all* beliefs regarding the real, because reality is defined in another connection as the object represented by a *true* opinion, and a true opinion is that which is fated to be agreed to after an investigation is complete. Reality then can consist only in certain selected beliefs. But if reality is this set of ultimately-adopted beliefs, what is truth itself? For truth has been defined as the beliefs which will be ultimately adopted.

In other words, when Peirce applies his method for clearness to the concept of reality, he reduces reality to truth. He identifies the two. Then there remains no independent realty which stands as a *check* on truth. And this was the postulate of his method of science.

Since the application of his own method for clearness eliminates reality, it looks as though Peirce must abandon either this method or the postulate of science. He cannot use both the method for clearness and the postulate of the method of science.

We must remember that Peirce was a pioneer in this movement. And in making the transition from the older form of thought, he occasionally uses a word both in the old sense and in the new. Such would seem to be his difficulty with the word 'reality', which he uses both in the newer sense which the method for clearness would show it to have, and in the old orthodox sense of something absolute. When he says "reality ... consists of the peculiar sensible effects which things partaking of it produce", he seems to have the two senses of the word in one sentence. Reality consists in sensible effects, or it is that which is produced somehow by means of our senses. But, when things *partake* of reality, reality exists in advance and produces those effects. Reality is conceived both as the things produced and as the producer of these things.

A somewhat similar difficulty occurs, as I may point out again in criticism, in the use of the words 'meaning' and 'belief'. Here the confusion is caused, not by using a word in two senses, as in the case of 'reality', but by using both the words 'meaning' and 'belief' in the same sense. Peirce defines both 'meaning' and 'belief' as a sum of habits, and indicates no difference between them.

Thus he says of meaning, "There is no distinction of meaning so fine as to consist in anything but a possible difference in practice". (293) "To develop its meaning, we have, therefore, simply to determine what habits it produces, for what a thing means is simply what habits it involves". (p. 292).

But he says similarly of belief, "Belief involves the establishment in our nature of a rule of action, or, say for short, of a habit". "Since belief is a rule for action, it is a new starting point for thought". "The essence of belief is the establishment of a habit, and different beliefs are distinguished by the different modes of action to which they give rise". (p. 291).

Now it will be agreed that instead of defining belief and meaning in terms of the same thing and thus identifying them, we ought sharply to distinguish between them. To have the meaning of a thing is not at all the same as to believe in it. Thus one may have clearly in mind the meaning of centaurs or of fairies or of any of the characters of mythology without in the slightest degree believing in them. Defining these things in terms of sensible effects, we could say that we know their meaning in the sense that we understand which sensible effects would be involved if they did exist. But to have a belief about them would mean that we would *expect* these sensible effects. In other words, a belief involves the possibility of fulfillment or frustration of expectation. To believe in anything is therefore a distinct step beyond understanding it.

In inserting these theories of reality and of belief in this discussion of a method for clear apprehension, Peirce is passing beyond a doctrine of clearness and involving himself in a doctrine of truth. We have seen that he does not seem to be able to maintain the postulated reality underlying his description of the scientific method for attaining truth. And it now seems that he is in equal difficulty with belief. If *meaning* is simply a sum of habits, belief is *not* simply a sum of habits, for the two are not the same. And if, as we have said, the quality that distinguishes belief from meaning is the fact that it involves expectation, then we appear to be on the verge of a new theory of truth,—a theory saying that truth is simply the fulfillment of these expectations.

Such, we may note, is the interpretation that Dewey puts upon the pragmatic method,—such is the theory of truth that he finds involved in it.

The interpretations of pragmatism which came particularly to the notice of Peirce, however, were those made by James and Schiller, and against these, we may say here, he made vigorous protest. These he regarded as perversions of his doctrine. And he was so desirous of indicating that his own theory of clearness involved for himself no such developments as these, that, in order to make the distinctions clear, he renamed his own doctrine.

His first article of dissent, appearing in The Monist in 1905, was directed mainly, however, against the looseness of popular usage. He traces briefly the doctrine's growth. Referring back to his original statement in 1878, he says of himself that he "framed the theory that a *conception*, that is, the rational purpose of a word or other expression, lies exclusively in its conceivable bearing upon the conduct of life; so that, since obviously nothing that might not result from experiment can have any direct bearing upon conduct, if one can define accurately all the conceivably experimental phenomena which the affirmation or denial of a concept could imply, one will have therein a complete definition of the concept, and *there is absolutely nothing more in it*. For this doctrine he [Peirce, now speaking of himself] invented the name of pragmatism…. His word 'pragmatism' has gained general recognition in a generalized sense that seems to argue power of growth and vitality. The famed psychologist, James, first took it up, seeing that his 'radical empiricism' substantially answered to the writer's definition, albeit with a certain difference in point of view. Next the admirably clear and brilliant thinker, Mr. Ferdinand C. S. Schiller, casting about for a more attractive name for the 'anthropomorphism' of his *Riddle of the Sphinx*, lit, in that most remarkable paper of his on Axioms as Postulates, upon the designation 'pragmatism', which in its original sense was in generic agreement with his own doctrine, for which he has since found the more appropriate specification 'humanism', while he still retains pragmatism in a somewhat wider sense. So far all went happily. But at present the word begins to be met with occasionally in the literary journals, where it gets abused in the merciless way that words have to expect when they fall into literary clutches. Sometimes the manners of the British have effloresced in scolding at the word as ill-chosen—ill-chosen, that is, to express some meaning that it was rather designed to exclude. So, then, the writer, finding his bantling 'pragmatism' so promoted, feels that it is time to kiss his child good-by and relinquish it in its higher destiny; while to serve the precise purpose of expressing the original definition, he begs to announce the birth of the word 'pragmaticism', which is ugly enough to be safe from kidnappers". (pp. 165-6).

Three years later Peirce published an article of much more outspoken protest, this time including in his repudiation the professional philosophers as well as the popularists. Writing for the Hibbert Journal (v.7) he states his case as follows:

"About forty years ago my studies of Kant, Berkeley, and others led me, after convincing myself that all thinking is performed in signs, and that mediation takes the form of dialogue, so that it is proper to speak of the 'meaning' of a concept, to conclude that to acquire full mastery of that meaning it is requisite, in the first place, to learn to recognize that concept under every disguise, through extensive familiarity with instances of it. But this, after all, does not imply any true understanding of it; so that it is further requisite that we should make an abstract logical analysis of it into its ultimate elements, or as complete an analysis as we can compass. But even so, we may still be without any living comprehension of it; and the only way to complete our knowledge of its nature is to discover and recognize just what habits of conduct a belief in the truth of the concept (of any conceivable subject, and under any conceivable circumstances) would reasonably develop; that is to say, what habits would ultimately result from a sufficient consideration of such truth. It is necessary to understand the word 'conduct', here, in the broadest sense. If, for example, the predication of a given concept were to lead to our admitting that a given form of reasoning concerning the subject of which it was affirmed was valid, when it would not otherwise be valid, the recognition of that effect in our reasoning would decidedly be a habit of conduct". (p.108).

After referring to his own expositions he continues, "... But in 1897 Professor James remodelled the matter, and transmogrified it into a doctrine of philosophy, some parts of which I highly approved, while other and more prominent parts I regarded, and still regard, as opposed to sound logic. About the same time Professor Papirie discovered, to the delight of the Pragmatist school, that this doctrine was incapable of definition, which would certainly seem to distinguish it from every other doctrine in whatever branch of science, I was coming to the conclusion that my poor little maxim should be called by another name; and I accordingly, in April 1905, renamed it Pragmaticism." (p.109).

"My original essay, having been written for a popular monthly, assumes, for no better reason than that real inquiry cannot begin until a state of real doubt arises, and ends as soon as a real Belief is attained, that a 'settlement of belief', or in other words, a *state of satisfaction*, is all that Truth, or the aim of inquiry, consists in. The reason I gave for this was so flimsy, while the inference was so nearly the gist of Pragmaticism, that I must confess the argument of that essay might be said with some justice to beg the question. The first part of the essay is occupied, however, with showing that, if Truth consists in satisfaction, it cannot be any *actual* satisfaction, but must be the satisfaction that would ultimately be found if the inquiry were pushed to its ultimate and indefeasible issue. This, I beg to point out, is a very different position from that of Mr. Schiller and the pragmatists of to-day.... Their avowedly undefinable position, if it be not capable of logical characterization, seems to me to be characterized by an angry hatred of strict logic, and even a disposition to rate any exact thought which interferes with their doctrine as all humbug. At the same time it seems to me clear that their approximate acceptance of the Pragmaticistic principle, and even that very casting aside of difficult distinctions (although I cannot approve of it), has helped them to a mightily clear discernment of some fundamental truths that other philosophers have seen but through a mist, or most of them not at all. Among such truths,—all of them old, of course, yet acknowledged by few—I reckon their denial of necessitarianism; their rejection of any 'consciousness' different from a visceral or other external sensation; their acknowledgment that there are, in a Pragmatistical sense, Real habits ... and their insistence upon interpreting all hypostatic abstractions in terms of what they *would* or *might* (not actually *will*) come to in the concrete. It seems to me a pity that they should allow a philosophy so instinct with life to become infected with seeds of death in such notions as that of the unreality of all ideas of infinity and that of the mutability of truth, and in such confusions of thought as that of active willing (willing to control thought, to doubt, and to weigh reasons) with willing not to exert the will (willing to believe)". (pp.111, 112).

The difference between the position of Peirce and of James may be stated in another way as constituted by the fact that James introduces the factor of *value* as a criterion for meaning and for truth, while for Peirce these elements did not enter the question at all. For James the value of a belief is an apparent evidence for its truth, while for Peirce value had no relation to truth. For an account of this development of the pragmatic doctrine we pass on now to a discussion of James.

CHAPTER II.
The Interpretation Given to Pragmatism by James.

James first uses the term 'pragmatism', as Peirce had done, to refer to a method for attaining clearness. When, in 1898, he brought again before the public the original article by Peirce, he was simply expounding the Peircian doctrine without making any attempt to pass beyond it. But, as we have just seen, he later gave it a construction, an interpretation as a theory of truth, with which its originator could not agree. In this chapter we may, therefore, look first at his exposition of the doctrine of clearness, and after that, in order to understand James' development of the doctrine into a theory of truth, we may turn back for a moment to some of his previous publications on the question of truth. It will then be possible to trace chronologically his developing attitude toward the truth controversy. From this we may pass finally to an indication of some of the difficulties in which he becomes involved. The most important of these, it may be said again, is that he construes the test of truth of an idea to be, not merely that the idea leads to expected consequences, but that it leads to predominantly desirable consequences. The outcomes which stand as evidence for truth are then not merely outcomes bringing fulfilled expectations but outcomes bringing happiness.

JAMES' EXPOSITION OF PEIRCE.

James in expounding the doctrine of Peirce explains the pragmatic principle as a method of investigating philosophic controversies, reducing them to essentials (clear meanings), and selecting those worthy of discussion.2 "Suppose", he says, "that there are two different philosophical definitions, or propositions, or maxims, or what not, which seem to contradict each other, and about which men dispute. If, by assuming the truth of the one, you can foresee no practical consequence to anybody, at any time or place, which is different from what you would foresee if you assumed the truth of the other, why then the difference between the two propositions is no real difference—it is only a specious and verbal difference, unworthy of future contention.... There can *be* no difference which does not *make* a difference—no difference in the abstract truth which does not express itself in a difference of concrete fact, and of conduct consequent upon that fact, imposed upon somebody, somehow, somewhere and somewhen.... The whole function of philosophy ought to be to find out what definite difference it would make to you and me, at definite instants of our life, if this world-formula or that world-formula be the one which is true". (p.675).

This doctrine is illustrated by using it to secure the essence of two philosophical questions, materialism vs. theism and the one *vs.* the many. If we suppose for an instant, he suggests, that this moment is the last moment of the universe's existence, there will be no *difference* between materialism and theism. All the effects that might be ascribed to either have come about.

"These facts are in, are bagged, are captured; and the good that's in them is gained, be the atom or be the God their cause." (p. 677). "The God, if there, has been doing just what the atom could do—appearing in the character of atoms, so to speak, and earning such gratitude as is due to atoms, and no more". Future good or ill is ruled out by postulate. Taken thus retrospectively, there could be no difference between materialism and theism.

But taken prospectively, they point to wholly different consequences. "For, according to the theory of mechanical evolution, the laws of redistribution of matter and motion, though they are certainly to thank for all the good hours which our organisms have ever yielded us and all the ideals which our minds now frame, are yet fatally certain to undo their work again, and to redissolve everything that they have evolved.... We make complaint of |materialism| for what it is *not*—not a permanent warrant for our more ideal interests, not a fulfiller of our remotest hopes.... Materialism means simply the denial that the moral order is eternal, and the cutting off of ultimate hopes; theism means the affirmation of an eternal moral order and the letting loose of hope. Surely here is an issue genuine enough for anyone who feels it....

"[And] if there be a God, it is not likely that he is confined solely to making differences in the world's latter end; he probably makes differences all along its course. Now the principle of practicalism says that that very meaning of the conception of God lies in the differences which must be made in experience if the conception be true. God's famous inventory of perfections, as elaborated by dogmatic theology, either means nothing, says our principle, or it implies certain definite things that we can feel and do at certain definite moments of our lives, things that we could not feel and should not do were no God present and were the business of the universe carried on by material atoms instead. So far as our conceptions of the Deity involve no such experiences, they are meaningless and verbal,—scholastic entities and abstractions, as the positivists say, and fit objects for their scorn. But so far as they do involve such definite experiences, God means something for us, and may be real". (pp.678-680).

The second illustration of the pragmatic principle—the supposed opposition between the One and the Many—may be treated more briefly. James suggests certain definite and practical sets of results in which to define 'oneness', and tries out the conception to see whether this result or that is what oneness means. He finds this method to clarify the difficulty here as well as in the previous case. In summarizing he says: "I have little doubt myself that this old quarrel might be completely smoothed out to the satisfaction of all claimants, if only the maxim of Peirce were methodically followed here. The current monism on the whole still keeps talking in too abstract a way. It says that the world must either be pure disconnectedness, no universe at all, or absolute unity. It insists that there is no stopping-place half-way. Any connection whatever, says this monism, is only possible if there be still more connection, until at last we are driven to admit the absolutely total connection required. But this absolutely total connection either means nothing, is the mere word 'one' spelt long, or else it means the sum of all the partial connections that can possibly be conceived. I believe that when we thus attack the question, and set ourselves to search for these possible connections, and conceive each in a definite and practical way, the dispute is already in a fair way to be settled beyond the chance of misunderstanding, by a compromise in which the Many and the One both get their lawful rights". (p. 685).

In concluding, James relates Peirce to the English Empiricists, asserting that it was they "who first introduced the custom of interpreting the meaning of conceptions by asking what differences they make for life.... The great English way of investigating a conception is to ask yourself right off, 'What is it known as? In what facts does it result? What is its *cash-value* in terms of particular experience? And what special difference would come into the world according as it were true or false?" Thus does Locke treat the conception of personal identity. What you mean by it is just your chain of memories, says he.... So Berkeley with his 'matter'. The cash-value of matter is just our physical sensations.... Hume does the same thing with causation. It is known as habitual antecedence.... Stewart and Brown, James Mill, John Mill, and Bain, have followed more or less consistently the same method; and Shadworth Hodgson has used it almost as explicitly as Mr. Peirce.... The short-comings and negations and the baldnesses of the English philosophers in question come, not from their eye to merely practical results, but solely from their failure to track the practical results completely enough to see how far they extend". (pp. 685-6).

It will be at once observed that James, as well as Peirce, is at this point saying nothing about a new doctrine of truth, but is concerning himself only with a new doctrine of clearness. Meaning and clearness of meanings are his only topics in this paper. Thus he states, "The only *meaning* of the conception of God lies in the differences which must be made in experience *if* the conception be true. God's famous inventory of perfection ... either *means* nothing, says our principle, or it implies certain definite things that we can feel and do at certain definite moments in our lives". And again in speaking of the pluralism-monism controversy, "Any connection whatever, says this monism, is only possible if there be still more connection, until at last we are driven to admit the absolutely total connection required. But this absolutely total connection either *means* nothing, is the mere word 'one' spelt long, or else it means the sum of all the partial connections...."

But as we all know, James did afterward embrace the new pragmatic theory of truth. While he did not in 1898 use the word pragmatism to designate anything except a new method for securing clearness, yet it can be shown that he had been developing another line of thought, since a much earlier date, which did lead quite directly toward the pragmatic theory of truth. It may be well at this point then to go back and trace the growth of this idea of truth through such writing as he had done before this time. It will be found, I think, that James' whole philosophic tendency to move away from the transcendental and unitary toward the particular was influencing him towards this new conception.

Development of the Doctrine through the Earlier Writings of James.

The first article which James wrote on truth, as he later states,[3] was entitled "The Function of Cognition", and was published in *Mind* in 1885. Commenting on this article in 1909 he asserts that many of the essential theses of the book "Pragmatism", published twenty-two years later, were already to be found here, and that the difference is mainly one of emphasis.[4]

This article attempts to give a description of knowing as it actually occurs,—not how it originated nor how it is antecedently possible.

The thesis is that an idea knows an external reality when it points to it, resembles it, and is able to affect it. The plan of exposition is to start with the simplest imaginable material and then gradually introduce additional matter as it is needed until we have cognition as it actually occurs. James postulates a single, momentarily-existing, floating feeling as the entire content, at the instant, of the universe. What, then, can this momentary feeling know? Calling it a 'feeling of q', it can be made any particular feeling (fragrance, pain, hardness) that the reader likes. We see, first, that the feeling cannot properly be said to know itself. There is no inner duality of the knower on the one hand and content or known on the other. "If the content of the feeling occurs nowhere else in the universe outside of the feeling itself, and perish with the feeling, common usage refuses to call it a reality, and brands it as a subjective feature of the feeling's constitution, or at most as the feeling's dream. For the feeling to be cognitive in the specific sense, then, it must be self-transcendent". And we must therefore "create a reality outside of it to correspond to the intrinsic quality q". This can stand as the first complication of that universe. Agreeing that the feeling cannot be said to know itself, under what conditions does it know the external reality? James replies, "If the newly-created reality *resemble* the feeling's quality q, I say that the feeling may be held by us to be *cognizant of that reality*". It may be objected that a momentary feeling cannot properly know a thing because it has no *time* to become aware of any of the *relations* of the thing. But this rules out only one of the kinds of knowledge, namely "knowledge about" the thing; knowledge as direct acquaintance remains. We may then assert that "if there be in the universe a q other than the q in the feeling the latter may have acquaintance with an entity ejective to itself; an acquaintance moreover, which, as mere acquaintance it would be hard to imagine susceptible either of improvement or increase, being in its way complete; and which would oblige us (so long as we refuse not to call acquaintance knowledge) to say not only that the feeling is cognitive, but that all qualities *of feeling, so long as there is anything outside of them which they resemble*, are feelings of qualities of existence, and perceptions of outward fact". But this would be true, as unexceptional rule, only in our artificially simplified universe. If there were a number of different q's for the feeling to resemble, while it meant only one of them, there would obviously be something more than resemblance in the case of the one which it did know. This fact, that resemblance is not enough in itself to constitute knowledge, can be seen also from remembering that many feelings which do resemble each other closely,—e. g., toothaches—do not on that account know each other. Really to know a thing, a feeling must not only resemble the thing, but must also be able to act on it. In brief, "the feeling of *q* knows whatever reality it resembles, and either directly or indirectly operates on. If it resemble without operating, it is a dream; if it operates without resembling, it is an error". Such is the formula for perceptual knowledge. Concepts must be reduced to percepts, after which the same rule holds. We may say, to make the formula complete, "A percept knows whatever reality it directly or indirectly operates on and resembles; a conceptual feeling, or thought, knows a reality, whenever it actually or potentially terminates in a percept that operates on, or resembles that reality, or is otherwise connected with it or with its context".

"The latter percept [the one to which the concept has been reduced] may be either sensation or sensorial idea; and when I say the thought must *terminate* in such a percept, I mean that it must ultimately be capable of leading up thereto,—by way of practical experience if the terminal feeling be a sensation; by way of logical or habitual suggestion, if it be only an image in the mind". "These percepts, these *termini*, these sensible things, these mere matters of acquaintance, are the only realities we ever directly know, and the whole history of our thought is the history of our substitution of one of them for the other, and the reduction of the substitute to the status of a conceptual sign. Condemned though they be by some thinkers, these sensations are the mother-earth, the anchorage, the stable rock, the first and last limits, the *terminus a quo* and the *terminus ad quem* of the mind. To find such sensational termini should be our aim with all our higher thought. They end discussion; they destroy the false conceit of knowledge; and without them we are all at sea with each other's meanings.... We can never be sure we understand each other till we are able to bring the matter to this test. This is why metaphysical discussions are so much like fighting with the air; they have no practical issue of a sensational kind. Scientific theories, on the other hand, always terminate in definite percepts. You can deduce a possible sensation from your theory and, taking me into your laboratory prove that your theory is true of my world by giving me the sensation then and there".

At this point James quotes, in substantiation, the following passage from Peirce's article of 1878: "There is no distinction in meaning so fine as to consist in anything but a possible difference in practice.... It appears, then, that the rule for attaining the highest grade of clearness of apprehension is as follows: Consider what effects, which might conceivably have practical bearings, we conceive the object of our conception to have. Then our conception of these effects is the whole of our conception of the object."

In this early paper of James' are to be found foreshadowings of pragmatism both as a method and as a theory of truth. Pragmatism as a method is shown in the whole discussion of the primacy of sensations and of the necessity for reducing conceptions to perceptions. This is exactly in line with the pragmatism proposed by Peirce in 1878 and here quoted from by James. Pragmatism as a theory of truth is anticipated by the proposal that the idea knows, and knows truly, the reality which it is able to make changes in. The idea *proves* its reference to a given reality by making these specified changes. It is antecedently true only if it can bring about these changes. The next step is to say that its truth *consists* in its ability to forecast and bring to pass these changes. Then we have pragmatism as a theory of truth. James did not take this step, as we shall see, until after 1904.

There is also a suggestion of the 'subjectivity' of James' later theory of truth, which would differentiate him even at this time from Peirce on the question of truth. He has said that a true idea must indeed resemble reality, but who, he asks, is to determine what is real? He answers that an idea is true when it resembles something which I, as critic, *think* to be reality. "When [the enquirer] finds that the feeling that he is studying contemplates what he himself regards as a reality he must of course admit the feeling itself to be truly cognitive". Peirce would say that the idea is not true unless it points to a reality that would be found by *all* investigators, quite irrespective of what the *one* person acting as critic may think. James and Pierce would therefore, begin to diverge even at this early date on the truth question. As to what constitutes clearness, they are in agreement.

Something of the same idea is stated again four years later in an article which appeared in Mind5 and which was republished the following year as a chapter of the Principles of Psychology.6 One passage will show the general trend; "A conception to prevail, must *terminate* in a world of orderly experience. A rare phenomenon, to displace frequent ones, must belong with others more frequent still. The history of science is strewn with wrecks and ruins of theory— essences and principles, fluids and forces—once fondly clung to, but found to hang together with no facts of sense. The exceptional phenomena solicit our belief in vain until such time as we chance to conceive of them as of kinds already admitted to exist. What science means by 'verification' is no more than this, that *no object of conception shall be believed which sooner or later has not some permanent object of sensation for its term*.... Sensible vividness or pungency is then the vital factor in reality when once the conflict between objects, and the connecting of them together in the mind, has begun." (Italics mine).

And in another connection he expresses the idea as follows: "Conceptual systems which neither began nor left off in sensations would be like bridges without piers. Systems about fact must plunge themselves into sensations as bridges plunge themselves into the rock. Sensations are the stable rock, the *terminus a quo* and the *terminus ad quem* of thought. To find such termini is our aim with all our theories—to conceive first when and where a certain sensation may be had and then to have it. Finding it stops discussion. Failure to find it kills the false conceit of knowledge. Only when you deduce a possible sensation for me from your theory, and give it to me when and where the theory requires, do I begin to be sure that your thought has anything to do with truth." (11:7).

In 1902 James contributed to the "Dictionary of Philosophy and Psychology" published by J. Mark Baldwin the following definition for Pragmatism.

"The doctrine that the whole 'meaning' of a conception expresses itself in practical consequences, consequences either in the shape of conduct to be recommended, or in that of experience to be expected, if the conception be true; which consequences would be different if it were untrue, and must be different from the consequences by which the meaning of other conceptions is in turn expressed. If a second conception should not appear to have either consequences, then it must really be only the first conception under a different name. In methodology it is certain that to trace and compare their respective consequences is an admirable way of establishing the different meanings of different conceptions".

It will be seem that James has not in 1902 differentiated between pragmatism as a method and as a theory of truth. Leaving out the one reference to truth, the definition is an excellent statement of the Peircian doctrine of clearness. This is especially to be noticed in the last two sentences, which are perfectly 'orthodox' statements of method alone.

In 1904 and 1905 James published two papers in Mind on the truth question. The first, "Humanism and Truth", may be called his 'border-line' article. In this he is attempting to give a sympathetic interpretation of the humanistic theory of truth—which he later said is exactly like his own—but is still making the interpretation as an outsider. In the second article he has definitely embraced the humanistic theory and is defending it.

The first article begins as follows:7 "Receiving from the editor of Mind an advance proof of Mr. Bradley's article for July on 'Truth and Practice', I understand this as a hint to me to join in the controversy over 'Pragmatism' which seems to have seriously begun. As my name has been coupled with the movement, I deem it wise to take the hint, the more so as in some quarters greater credit has been given me than I deserve, and probably undeserved discredit in other quarters falls also to my lot.

"First, as to the word 'pragmatism'. I myself have only used the term to indicate a method of carrying on abstract discussion. The serious meaning of a concept, says Mr. Peirce, lies in the concrete difference to someone which its being true will make. Strive to bring all debated questions to that 'pragmatic' test, and you will escape vain wrangling: if it can make no practical difference which of two statements be true, then they are really one statement in two verbal forms; if it can make no practical difference whether a given statement be true or false, then the statement has no real meaning. In neither case is there anything fit to quarrel about; we may save our breath, and pass to more important things.

"All that the pragmatic method implies, then, is that truths should *have* practical consequences. In England the word has been used more broadly, to cover the notion that the truth of any statement consists in the consequences, and particularly in their being good consequences. Here we get beyond affairs of method altogether; and since this pragmatism and the wider pragmatism are so different, and both are important enough to have different names, I think that Mr. Schiller's proposal to call the wider pragmatism by the name of 'Humanism' is excellent and ought to be adopted. The narrower pragmatism may still be spoken of as the 'pragmatic method'.

"If further egotism be in order. I may say that the account of truth given by Messrs. Sturt and Schiller and by Professor Dewey and his school … goes beyond any theorizing which I personally had ever indulged in until I read their writings. After reading these, *I feel almost sure that these authors are right in their main contentions*, but the originality is wholly theirs, and I can hardly recognize in my own humble doctrine that concepts are teleological instruments anything considerable enough to warrant my being called, as I have been, the 'father' of so important a movement forward in philosophy".8 (Italic mine).

"I think that a decided effort at a sympathetic mental play with humanism is the provisional attitude to be recommended to the reader.

"*When I find myself playing sympathetically with humanism*, something like what follows is what I end by conceiving it to mean". (Italics mine).

Such is the conservative tone in which the article is begun. Yet before it is ended we find these passages: "It seems obvious that the pragmatic account of all this routine of phenomenal knowledge is accurate". (p.468). "The humanism, for instance, which I see and try so hard to defend, is the completest truth attained from my point of view up to date". (p.472).

In a supplementary article, "Humanism and Truth Once More", published a few months later in answer to questions prompted by this one, the acceptance of humanism is entirely definite. And here James finds that he has been advocating the doctrine for several years. He says, "I myself put forth on several occasions a radically pragmatist account of knowledge". (Mind, v. 14, p. 196). And again he remarks, "When following Schiller and Dewey, I define the true as that which gives the maximal combination of satisfaction …". (p.196).

THE THEORY OF TRUTH IN 'PRAGMATISM' AND 'THE MEANING OF TRUTH'.

In 1907 when he published his book "Pragmatism", James, as we all know, was willing to accept the new theory of truth unreservedly. The hesitating on the margin, the mere interpreting of other's views, are things of the past. From 1907 James' position toward pragmatism as a truth-theory is unequivocal.

Throughout the book, as I should like to point out, James is using 'pragmatism' in two senses, and 'truth' in two senses. The two meanings of pragmatism he recognizes himself, and points out clearly the difference between pragmatism as a method for attaining clearness in our ideas and pragmatism as a theory of the truth or falsity of those ideas. But the two meanings of 'truth' he does not distinguish. And it is here that he differs from Dewey, as we shall presently see. He differed from Peirce on the question of the meaning of pragmatism—as to whether it could be developed to include a doctrine of truth as well as of clearness. He differs from Dewey on the question of 'truth'—as to whether truth shall be used in both of the two specified senses or only in one of them.

The Ambiguity of 'Satisfaction'—The double meaning of truth in James' writing at this date may be indicated in this way: While truth is to be defined in terms of satisfaction, what is satisfaction? Does it mean that I am to be satisfied *of* a certain quality in the idea, or that I am to be satisfied *by* it? In other words, is the criterion of truth the fact that the idea leads as it promised or is it the fact that its leading, whether just as it promised or not, is desirable? Which, in short, are we to take as truth,—fulfilled expectations or value of results?

It is in failing to distinguish between these two that James involves himself, I believe, in most of his difficulties, and it is in the recognition and explicit indication of this difference that Dewey differentiates himself from James. We may pass on to cite specific instances in which James uses each of these criteria. We will find, of course, that there are passages which can be interpreted as meaning either value or fulfillment, but there are many in which the use of value as a criterion seems unmistakable.

The following quotations may be instanced: "If theological views prove to have value for concrete life, they will be true, for pragmatism, in the sense of being good for so much. For how much more they are true, will depend entirely on their relation to the other truths that have also to be acknowledged". For example, in so far as the Absolute affords comfort, it is not sterile; "it has that amount of value; it performs a concrete function. I myself ought to call the Absolute true 'in so far forth', then; and I unhesitatingly now do so". (p.72).

"On pragmatic principles, if the hypothesis of God works satisfactorily in the widest sense of the word, it is true. Now whatever its residual difficulties may be, experience shows that it certainly does work, and that the problem is to build out and determine it so that it will combine satisfactorily with all the other working truths". (p. 299).

"The true is the name for whatever proves itself to be good in the way of belief, and good, too, for definite, assignable reasons". (p. 76).

"Empirical psychologists ... have denied the soul, save as the name for verifiable cohesions in our inner life. They redescend into the stream of experience with it, and cash it into so much small-change value in the way of 'ideas' and their connections with each other. The soul is good or *'true'* for just so much, but no more". (p. 92, italics mine).

"Since almost any object may some day become temporarily important, the advantage of having a stock of extra truths, of ideas that shall be true of merely possible situations, is obvious.... Whenever such extra truths become practically relevant to one of our emergencies, it passes from cold storage to do work in the world and our belief in it grows active. You can say of it then either that *'it is useful because it is true' or that it is 'true because it is useful'. Both these phrases mean exactly the same thing*.... From this simple cue pragmatism gets her general notion of truth as something essentially bound up with the way in which one moment in our experience may lead us towards other moments *which it will be worth while to have been led to*. Primarily, and on the common-sense level, the truth of a state of mind means this function of *a leading that is worth while*". (pp. 204-205, italics mine).

"To 'agree' in the widest sense with reality can only mean to be guided either straight up to it or into its surroundings, or to be put into such working touch with it as to handle either it or something connected with it better than if we disagreed. *Better either intellectually or practically!*... An idea that helps us to deal, whether *practically or intellectually*, with either reality or its belongings, that doesn't entangle our progress in frustrations, that fits, in fact, and adapts our life to the reality's whole setting, will——hold true of that reality". (pp. 212-213).

"'The true', to put it very briefly, is only the expedient in the way of our thinking, just as the 'right' is only the expedient in the way of our behaving. *Expedient in almost any fashion*; and expedient in the long run and on the whole of course". (p. 222).

We may add a passage with the same bearing, from "The Meaning of Truth". In this quotation James is retracting the statement made in the University of California Address that without the future there is no difference between theism and materialism. He says: "Even if matter could do every outward thing that God does, the idea of it would not work as satisfactorily, because the chief call for a God on modern men's part is for a being who will inwardly recognize them and judge them sympathetically. Matter disappoints this craving of our ego, and so God remains for most men the truer hypothesis, and indeed remain so for definite pragmatic reasons". (p. 189, notes).

The contrast between 'intellectual' and 'practical' seems to make his position certain. If truth is tested by practical workings, *as contrasted with* intellectual workings, it cannot be said to be limited to fulfilled expectation.

The statement that the soul is good *or* true shows the same thing. The relation of truth to extraneous values is here beyond question. The other passages all bear, more or less obviously, in the same direction.

As James keeps restating his position, there are many of the definitions that could be interpreted to mean either values or fulfillments, and even a few which seem to refer to fulfillment alone. The two following examples can be taken to mean either:

"'Truth' in our ideas and beliefs means ... that ideas (which themselves are but parts of our experience) become true just in so far as they help us to get into satisfactory relation with other parts of our experience, to summarize them and get about among them by conceptual short-cuts instead of following the interminable succession of particular phenomena. Any idea upon which we can ride, so to speak; any idea that will carry us prosperously from one part of our experience to any other part, linking things satisfactorily, working securely, simplifying, saving labor, is true for just so much, true in so far forth, true instrumentally". (p.58).

"A new opinion counts as true just in proportion as it gratifies the individual's desire to assimilate the novel in his experience to his beliefs in stock. It must both lean on old truth and grasp new fact; and its success ... in doing this, is a matter for individual appreciation. When old truth grows, then, by new truth's addition, it is for subjective reasons. We are in the process and obey the reasons. The new idea is truest which performs most felicitously its function of satisfying this double urgency. It makes itself true, gets itself classed as true, by the way it works." (p.64).

But we can turn from these to a paragraph in which truth seems to be limited to fulfilled expectations alone.

"True ideas are those which we can assimilate, validate, corroborate, and verify. False ideas are those which we cannot. That is the practical difference it makes to us to have true ideas; that, therefore, is the meaning of truth, for it is all that truth is known as....

"But what do validation and verification themselves pragmatically mean? They again signify certain practical consequences of the verified and validated idea.... They head us ... through the acts and other ideas which they instigate, into or up to, or towards, other parts of experience with which we feel all the while ... that the original ideas remain in agreement. The connections and transitions come to us from point to point as being progressive, harmonious, satisfactory. This function of agreeable leading is what we mean by an idea's verification". (pp.201-202).

The Relation of Truth to Utility—It seems certain from the foregoing that James means, at least at certain times, to define the true in terms of the valuable. Satisfaction he is using as satisfaction *by* rather than satisfaction *of*. As we have pointed out, one may be satisfied of the correctness of one's idea without being at all satisfied by it. This distinction has been most clearly set forth by Boodin, in his discussion of 'What pragmatism is not', in the following words: "The truth satisfaction may run counter to any moral or esthetic satisfaction in the particular case. It may consist in the discovery that the friend we had backed had involved us in financial failure, that the picture we had bought from the catalogue description is anything but beautiful. But we are no longer uncertain as regards the truth. Our restlessness, so far as that particular curiosity is concerned, has come to an end".9

It is clear then, that the discovery of truth is not to be identified with a predominantly satisfactory state of mind at the moment. Our state of mind at the moment may have only a grain of satisfaction, yet this is of so unique a kind and so entirely distinguishable from the other contents of the mind that it is perfectly practicable as a criterion. It is simply "the cessation of the irritation of a doubt", as Peirce puts it, or the feeling that my idea has led as it promised. The feeling of fulfilled expectation is thus a very distinct and recognizable *part* of the whole general feeling commonly described as 'satisfaction'. When 'utility' in our ideas, therefore, means a momentary feeling of dominant satisfaction, truth cannot be identified with it.

And neither, as I wish now to point out, can truth be identified with utility when utility means a long-run satisfactoriness, or satisfactoriness of the idea for a considerable number of people through a considerable period of time. The same objection arises here which we noted a moment ago—that the satisfaction may be quite indifferent to the special satisfaction arising from tests. As has been often shown, many ideas are satisfactory for a long period of time simply because they are *not* subjected to tests. "A hope is not a hope, a fear is not a fear, once either is recognized as unfounded.... A delusion is delusion only so long as it is not known to be one. A mistake can be built upon only so long as it is not suspected".

Some actual delusions which were not readily subjected to tests have been long useful in this way. "For instance, basing ourselves on Lafcadio Hearn, we might quite admit that the opinions summed up under the title 'Ancestor-Worship' had been ... 'exactly what was required' by the former inhabitants of Japan". "It was good for primitive man to believe that dead ancestors required to be fed and honored ... because it induced savages to bring up their offspring instead of letting it perish. But although it was useful to hold that opinion, the opinion was false". "Mankind has always wanted, perhaps always required, and certainly made itself, a stock of delusions and sophisms".10

Perhaps we would all agree that the belief that 'God is on our side' has been useful to the tribe holding it. If has increased zeal and fighting efficiency tremendously. But since God can't be on both sides, the belief of one party to the conflict is untrue, no matter how useful. To believe that (beneficial) tribal customs are enforced by the tribal gods is useful, but if the tribal gods are non-existent the belief is false. The beautiful imaginings of poets are sometimes useful in minimizing and disguising the hard and ugly reality, but when they will not test out they cannot be said because of their beauty or desirability to be true.

We must conclude then, that some delusions are useful. And we may go on and question James' identification of truth and utility from another point of view. Instead of agreeing that true ideas and useful ideas are the same, we have shown that some useful ideas are false: but the converse is also demonstrable, that some true ideas are useless.

There are formulas in pure science which are of no use to anyone outside the science because their practical bearings, if such there be, have not yet been discovered, and are of no use to the scientist himself because, themselves the products of deduction, they as yet suggest nothing that can be developed farther from them. While these formulas may later be found useful in either of these senses—for 'practical demands' outside the science, or as a means to something else within the science—they are now already true quite apart from utility, because they will test out by fulfilling expectations.

Knowledge that is not useful is most striking in relation to 'vice'. One may have a true idea as to how to lie and cheat, may know what cheating is and how it is done, and yet involve both himself and others in most *un*satisfactory consequences. The person who is attempting to stop the use of liquor, and who to this end has located in a 'dry' district, may receive correct information as to the location of a 'blind-tiger'—information which while true may bring about his downfall. Knowledge about any form of vice, true knowledge that can be tested out, may upon occasion be harmful to any extent we like.

We may conclude this section by citing a paragraph which will show the fallacious reasoning by which James came to identify the truth and the utility of ideas. At one point in replying to a criticism he says: "I can conceive no other objective *content* to the notion of an ideally perfect truth than that of penetration into [a completely satisfactory] terminus, nor can I conceive that the notion would ever have grown up, or that true ideas would ever have been sorted out from false or idle ones, save for the greater sum of satisfactions, intellectual or practical, which the truer ones brought with them. Can we imagine a man absolutely satisfied with an idea and with all his relations to his other ideas and to his sensible experiences, who should yet *not* take its content as a true account of reality? The *matter* of the true is thus absolutely identical with the matter of the satisfactory. You may put either word first in your way of talking; but leave out that whole notion of satisfactory working or leading (which is the essence of my pragmatic account) and call truth a static, logical relation, independent even of possible leadings or satisfactions, and it seems to me that you cut all ground from under you". (Meaning of Truth, p. 160).11

Now it is to be observed that this paragraph contains at least three logical fallacies. In the first sentence there is a false assumption, namely that 'all that survives is valuable'. 'Then', we are given to understand, 'since true ideas survive, they must be valuable'. No biologist would agree to this major premise. 'Correlation' preserves many things that are not valuable, as also do other factors.

In the second sentence there is an implied false conversion. The second sentence says, in substance, that all true ideas are satisfactory (valuable). This is supposed to prove the assertion of the first sentence, namely, that all satisfactory (valuable) ideas are true.

In the last sentence there is a false disjunction. Truth, it is stated, must either be satisfactory (valuable) working, or a static logical relation. We have tried to show that it may simply mean reliable working or working that leads as it promised. This may be neither predominantly valuable working nor a static logical relation.

The Relation of Satisfaction to Agreement and Consistency.—James continually reasserts that he has 'remained an epistemological realist', that he has 'always postulated an independent reality', that ideas to be true must 'agree with reality', etc.12

Reality he defines most clearly as follows:

"'Reality' is in general what truths have to take account of....

"The first part of reality from this point of view is the flux of our sensations. Sensations are forced upon us.... Over their nature, order and quantity we have as good as no control....

"The second part of reality, as something that our beliefs must also take account of, is the *relations* that obtain between their copies in our minds. This part falls into two sub-parts: (1) the relations that are mutable and accidental, as those of date and place; and (2) those that are fixed and essential because they are grounded on the inner nature of their terms. Both sorts of relation are matters of immediate perception. Both are 'facts'....

"The third part of reality, additional to these perceptions (tho largely based upon them), is the *previous truths* of which every new inquiry takes account". (Pragmatism, p. 244).

An idea's agreement with reality, or better with all those parts of reality, means a satisfactory relation of the idea to them. Relation to the sensational part of reality is found satisfactory when the idea leads to it without jar or discord. "... What do the words verification and validation themselves pragmatically mean? They again signify certain practical consequences of the verified and validated idea. It is hard to find any one phrase that characterizes these consequences better than the ordinary agreement-formula—just such consequences being what we have in mind when we say that our ideas 'agree' with reality. They lead us, namely, through the acts and other ideas which they instigate, into and up to, or towards, other parts of experience with which we feel all the while ... that the original ideas remain in agreement. The connections and transitions come to us from point to point as being progressive, harmonious, satisfactory. This function of agreeable leading is what we mean by an idea's verification". (Pragmatism, pp. 201-2).

An idea's relation to the other parts of reality is conceived more broadly. Thus pragmatism's "only test of probable truth is what works best in the way of leading us, what fits every part of life best and combines with the collectivity of life's demands, nothing being omitted. If theological ideas should do this, if the notion of God, in particular, should prove to do it, how could pragmatism possibly deny God's existence? She could see no meaning in treating as 'not true' a notion that was pragmatically so successful. What other kind of truth could there be, for her, than all this *agreement with concrete reality*"? (Pragmatism, p. 80, italics mine). Agreement with reality here means ability to satisfy the sum of life's demands.

James considers that this leaves little room for license in the choice of our beliefs. "Between the coercions of the sensible order and those of the ideal order, our mind is thus wedged tightly". "Our (any) theory must mediate between all previous truths and certain new experiences. It must derange common sense and previous belief as little as possible, and it must lead to some sensible terminus or other that can be verified exactly. To 'work' means both these things; and the squeeze is so tight that there is little loose play for any hypothesis. Our theories are thus wedged and controlled as nothing else is". "Pent in, as the pragmatist more than anyone else sees himself to be, between the whole body of funded truths squeezed from the past and the coercions of the world of sense about him, who so well as he feels the immense pressure of objective control under which our minds perform their operations". (Pragmatism, pp. 211, 217, 233).

Now on the contrary it immediately occurs to a reader that if reality be simply "what truths have to take account of", and if taking-account-of merely means agreeing in such a way as to satisfy "the collectivity of life's demands", then the proportion in which these parts of reality will count will vary enormously. One person may find the 'previous-truths' part of reality to make such a strong 'demand' that he will disregard 'principles' or reasoning almost entirely.

Another may disregard the 'sensational' part of reality, and give no consideration whatever to 'scientific' results. These things, in fact, are exactly the things that do take place. The opinionated person, the crank, the fanatic, as well as the merely prejudiced, all refuse to open their minds and give any particular consideration to such kinds of evidence. There is therefore a great deal of room for license, and a great deal of license practiced, when the agreement of our ideas with reality means nothing more than their satisfactoriness to our lives' demands.

How James fell into this error is shown, I believe, by his overestimation of the common man's regard for truth, and especially for consistency. Thus he remarks: "As we humans are constituted in point of fact, we find that to believe in other men's minds, in independent physical realities, in past events, in eternal logical relations, is satisfactory.... Above all we find *consistency* satisfactory, consistency between the present idea and the entire rest of our mental equipment...." "After man's interest in breathing freely, the greatest of all his interests (because it never fluctuates or remits, as most of his physical interests do), is his interest in *consistency*, in feeling that what he now thinks goes with what he thinks on other occasions". (Meaning of Truth, pp. 192, 211).

The general method of James on this point, then, is to define truth in terms of satisfaction and then to try to show that these satisfactions cannot be secured illegitimately. That is, that we *must* defer to experimental findings, to consistency, and to other *checks* on opinion. Consistency must be satisfactory because people are so constituted as to find it so. Agreement with reality, where reality means epistemological reality, is satisfactory for the same reason. And agreement with reality, where reality includes in addition principles and previous truths, must be satisfactory because agreement in this case merely means such taking-account-of as will satisfy the greater proportion of the demands of life. In other words, by defining agreement in this case in terms of satisfactions, he makes it certain that agreement and satisfaction will coincide by the device of arguing in a circle. It turns out that, from over-anxiety to assure the coincidence of agreement and satisfaction, he entirely loses the possibility of using reality and agreement with reality in the usual sense of checks on satisfactions.

CHAPTER III.
The Pragmatic Doctrine as Set Forth by Dewey.

The position of Dewey is best represented in his paper called "The Experimental Theory of Knowledge".13 In the method of presentation, this article is much like James' account "The Function of Cognition". Both assume some simple type of consciousness and study it by gradually introducing more and more complexity. In aim, also, the two are similar, for the purpose of each is simply to describe. Dewey attempts here to tell of a knowing just as one describes any other object, concern, or event. "What we want", he announces "is just something which takes itself for knowledge, rightly or wrongly".

Let us suppose, then, that we have simply a floating odor. If this odor starts changes that end in picking and enjoying a rose, what sort of changes must these be to involve some where within their course that which we call knowledge?

Now it can be shown, first, that there is a difference between knowing and mere presence in consciousness. If the smell is simply displaced by a felt movement, and this in turn is displaced by the enjoyment of the rose, in such a way that there is no experience of connection between the three stages of the process,—that is, without the appearance of memory or anticipation,—then "such an experience neither is, in whole or in part, a knowledge". "Acquaintance is presence honored by an escort; presence is introduced as familiar, or an association springs up to greet it. Acquaintance always implies a little friendliness; a trace of re-knowing, of anticipatory welcome or dread of the trait to follow.... To be a smell (or anything else) is one thing, to be *known* as a smell, another; to be a 'feeling' is one thing, to be *known* as a 'feeling' is another. The first is thinghood; existence indubitable, direct; in this way all things *are* that are in 'consciousness' at all. The second is *reflected* being, things indicating and calling for other things— something offering the possibility of truth and hence of falsity. The first is genuine immediacy; the second (in the instance discussed) a pseudo-immediacy, which in the same breath that it proclaims its immediacy smuggles in another term (and one which is unexperienced both in itself and in its relation) the subject of 'consciousness', to which the immediate is related.... To be acquainted with a thing is to be assured (from the standpoint of the experience itself) that it is of such and such a character; that it will behave, if given an opportunity, in such and such a way; that the obviously and flagrantly present trait is associated with fellow traits that will show themselves if the leading of the present trait is followed out. To be acquainted is to anticipate to some extent, on the basis of previous experience". (pp. 81, 82).

Besides mere existence, there is another type of experience which is often confused with knowledge,—a type which Dewey calls the 'cognitive' as distinct from genuine knowledge or the 'cognitional'. In this experience "we retrospectively attribute intellectual force and function to the smell". This involves memory but not anticipation. As we look back from the enjoyment of the rose, we can say that in a sense the odor meant the rose, even though it led us here blindly. That is, if the odor suggests the finding of its cause, without specifying what the cause is, and if we then search about and find the rose, we can say that the odor meant the rose in the sense that it actually led to the discovery of it. "Yet the smell is not cognitional because it did not knowingly intend to mean this, but is found, after the event, to have meant it". (p. 84).

Now, "before the category of confirmation or refutation can be introduced, there must be something which *means* to mean something". Let us therefore introduce a further complexity into the illustration. Let us suppose that the smell occurs at a later date, and is then "aware of something else which it means, which it intends to effect by an operation incited by it and without which its own presence is abortive, and, so to say, unjustified, senseless". Here we have something "which is contemporaneously aware of meaning something beyond itself, instead of having this meaning ascribed to it by another at a later period. *The odor knows the rose, the rose is known by the odor*, and the import of each term is constituted by the relationship in which it stands to the other". (p. 88). This is the genuine 'cognitional' experience.

When the odor recurs 'cognitionally', both the odor and the rose are present in the same experience, though both are not present in the same way. "Things can be presented as absent, just as they can be presented as hard or soft". The enjoyment of the rose is present as *going* to be there in the same way that the odor is. "The situation is inherently an uneasy one—one in which everything hangs upon the performance of the operation indicated; upon the adequacy of movement as a connecting link, or real adjustment of the thing meaning and the thing meant. Generalizing from this instance, we get the following definition: An experience is a knowledge, if in its quale there is an experienced distinction and connection of two elements of the following sort: one means or intends the presence of the other in the same fashion in which it itself is already present, while the other is that which, while not present in the same fashion, must become present if the meaning or intention of its companion or yoke-fellow is to be fulfilled through the operation it sets up". (p. 90).

Now in the transformation from this tensional situation into a harmonious situation, there is an experience either of fulfilment or disappointment. If there is a disappointment of expectation, this may throw one back in reflection upon the original situation. The smell, we may say, seemed to mean a rose, yet it did not in fact lead to a rose. There is something else which enters in. We then begin an investigation. "Smells may become the object of knowledge. They may take, *pro tempore*, the place which the rose formerly occupied. One may, that is, observe the cases in which the odors mean other things than just roses, may voluntarily produce new cases for the sake of further inspection; and thus account for the cases where meanings had been falsified in the issue; discriminate more carefully the peculiarities of those meanings which the event verified, and thus safeguard and bulwark to some extent the employing of similar meanings in the future". (p. 93). When we reflect upon these fulfilments or refusals, we find in them a quality "quite lacking to them in their immediate occurrence as just fulfilments and disappointments",—the quality of affording assurance and correction. "Truth and falsity are not properties of any experience or thing, in and of itself or in its first intention; but of things where the problem of assurance consciously enters in. Truth and falsity present themselves as significant facts only in situations in which specific meanings and their already experienced fulfilments and non-fulfilments are intentionally compared and contrasted with reference to the question of the worth, as to the reliability of meaning, of the given meaning or class of meanings. Like knowledge itself, truth is an experienced relation of things, and it has no meaning outside of such relation". (p. 95).

Though this paper is by title a discussion of a theory of knowledge, we may find in this last paragraph a very clear relating of the whole to a theory of truth. If we attempt to differentiate in this article between knowledge and truth, we find that while Dewey uses 'knowledge' to refer either to the prospective or to the retrospective end of the experimental experience, he evidently intends to limit truth to the retrospective or confirmatory end of the experience. When he says, "Truth and falsity are not properties of any experience or thing in and of itself or in its first intention, but of things where the problem of assurance consciously enters in. Truth and falsity present themselves as significant facts only in situations in which specific meanings and their already experienced fulfilments are intentionally compared and contrasted with reference to the question of the worth, as to reliability of meaning, of the given meaning or class of meanings", it seems that truth is to be confined to retrospective experience. The truth of an idea means that it allows one at its fulfilment to look back at its former meaning and think of it as now confirmed. The difference between knowledge and truth is then a difference in the time at which the developing experience is examined. If one takes the experience at the appearance of the knowing odor, he gets acquaintance; if one takes it at the stage at which it has developed into a confirmation, he gets truth. Knowledge may be either stage of the experience of verification, but truth is confined to the later, confirmatory, stage.

Truth, then, is simply a matter of confirmation of prediction or of fulfilment of expectation. An idea is made true by leading as it promised. And an idea is made false when it leads to refutation of expectation. There seems to be no necessity here for an absolute reality for the ideas to conform to, or 'correspond' to, for truth is a certain kind of relation between the ideas themselves—the relation, namely, of leading to fulfilment of expectations.

CONTRAST BETWEEN JAMES AND DEWEY.

If, now, we wish to bring out the difference between the account of truth which we have just examined and the account that is given by James, we will find the distinction quite evident. Truth, for Dewey, is that relation which arises when, at an experience of fulfilment, one looks back to the former experience and thinks of its leading as now confirmed. An idea is true, therefore, when we can refer back to it in this way and say, "That pointing led me to this experience, as it said it would". The pointing, by bringing a fulfilment, is *made* true—at this point of confirmation it *becomes* true.

Since a true idea is defined, then, as one which leads as it promised, it is obvious that truth will not be concerned in any way with incidental or accidental *values* which might be led to by the idea. It has no relation to whether the goal is *worth while* being led to or not. James speaks of truth as a leading that is worth while. For Dewey the goal may be valuable, useless, or even pernicious,—these are entirely irrelevant to truth, which is determined solely by the fact that the idea leads *as it promised.*

The existence of this distinction was pointed out, after the appearance of James' "Pragmatism", by Dewey himself.14 After a careful discussion of some other points of difference, he says of this matter of the place of the value of an idea in reference to its truth: "We have the theory that ideas as ideas are always working hypotheses concerning attaining particular empirical results, and are tentative programs (or sketches of method) for attaining them. If we stick consistently to this notion of ideas, only consequences which are actually produced by the working of the idea in cooperation with, or application to, prior realities are good consequences in the specific sense of good which is relevant to establishing the truth of an idea. This is, at times, unequivocally recognized by Mr. James.... But at other times any good that flows from acceptance of a belief is treated as if it were an evidence, *in so far*, of the truth of the idea. This holds particularly when theological notions are under consideration. Light would be thrown upon how Mr. James conceives this matter by statements from him on such points as these: If ideas terminate in good consequences, but yet the goodness of the consequence was no part of the intention of the idea, does the goodness have any verifying force? If the goodness of consequences arises from the context of the idea rather than from the idea itself, does it have any verifying force? If an idea leads to consequences which are good in the *one* respect only of fulfilling the intent of the idea, (as when one drinks a liquid to test the idea that it is a poison), does the badness of the consequences in every other respect detract from the verifying force of these consequences?

"Since Mr. James has referred to me as saying 'truth is what gives satisfaction' (p. 234), I may remark ... that I never identified *any* satisfaction with the truth of an idea, save *that* satisfaction which arises when the idea as working hypothesis or tentative method is applied to prior existences in such a way as to fulfil what it intends....

"When he says ... of the idea of an absolute, 'so far as it affords such comfort it surely is not sterile, it has that amount of value; it performs a concrete function. As a good pragmatist I ought to call the absolute true *in so far forth* then; and I unhesitatingly now do so', the doctrine seems to be unambiguous: that *any* good, consequent upon acceptance of belief, is, in so far forth, a warrant for truth. Of course Mr. James holds that this 'in so far' goes a very small way.... But even the slightest concession, is, I think, non-pragmatic unless the satisfaction is relevant to the idea as intent. Now the satisfaction in question comes not from the *idea as idea*, but from its acceptance *as true*. Can a satisfaction dependent upon an assumption that an idea is already true be relevant to testing the truth of an idea? And can an idea, like that of the absolute, which, if true, 'absolutely' precludes any appeal to consequences as test of truth, be confirmed by use of the pragmatic test without sheer self-contradiction"?15 "An explicit statement as to whether the carrying function, the linking of things, is satisfactory and prosperous and hence true in so far as it executes the intent of the idea; or whether the satisfaction and prosperity reside in the material consequences on their own account and in that aspect make the idea true, would, I am sure, locate the point at issue and economize and fructify future discussion. At present pragmatism is accepted by those whose own notions are thoroughly rationalistic in make-up as a means of refurbishing, galvanizing, and justifying those very notions. It is rejected by non-rationalists (empiricists and naturalistic idealists) because it seems to them identified with the notion that pragmatism holds that the desirability of certain beliefs overrides the question of the meaning of the idea involved in them and the existence of objects denoted by them. Others (like myself) who believe thoroughly in pragmatism as a method of orientation as defined by Mr. James, and who would apply the method to the determination of the meaning of objects, the intent and worth of ideas as ideas, and to the human and moral value of beliefs, when these problems are carefully distinguished from one another, do not know whether they are pragmatists or not, because they are not sure whether the 'practical', in the sense of the desirable facts which define the worth of a belief, is confused with the practical as an attitude imposed by objects, and with the practical as a power and function of idea to effect changes in prior existences. Hence the importance of knowing what pragmatism means by practical....

"I would do Mr. James an injustice, however, to stop here. His real doctrine, I think, is that a belief is true when it satisfies *both* the personal needs *and* the requirements of objective things. Speaking of pragmatism, he says, 'Her only test of probable truth is what works best in the way of *leading us*, what fits every part of life best *and combines with the collectivity of experience's demands*, nothing being omitted'. And again, 'That new idea is truest which performs most felicitously its function of satisfying *our double urgency*'. (p. 64). It does not appear certain from the context that this 'double urgency' is that of the personal and the objective demands, but it is probable.... On this basis, the 'in so far forth' of the truth of the absolute because of the comfort it supplies, means that *one* of the two conditions which need to be satisfied has been met, so that if the absolute met the other one also it would be quite true. I have no doubt that this is Mr. James' meaning, and it sufficiently safeguards him from charges that pragmatism means that anything that is agreeable is true. At the same time, I do not think, in logical strictness, that satisfying one of two tests, when satisfaction of both is required, can be said to constitute a belief true even 'in so far forth'".

CHAPTER IV.
Summary and Conclusion.

Writing as a scientist and publishing his work in a scientific journal, Peirce proposed in 1878 a new method for making our ideas clear. He was attempting a description of the logic of the sciences. He believed himself to be showing how the greatest of our modern thinkers do make clear to themselves their ideas of the objects with which they work. The meaning of anything, said Peirce, consists in the actual or possible effects which it might produce. Our idea of the thing is clear when we have in mind these sensible effects. This theory of clearness he called pragmatism.

No one, it seems, paid any especial attention to this theory at the time. But twenty years later James brought the subject to the forefront of discussion by explaining it anew in his exceptionally lucid way and by making a particular application of it to religion. But for James the method for clearness very soon grew into a new theory of truth, and in this way, in spite of the fact that the method had been proposed by a scientist as a description of the procedure of science, he seems to have lost for it the support of science. The reason for this outcome was his introduction of value as a criterion for truth. This, James recognizes, was counter to all the scientific ideals of many of the workers in science, for the essence of their procedure, as they saw it, was to put all desire as to outcomes behind them and to try to find out how things actually prove or test out to be, quite apart from how we would like them to be. To introduce the general value of an outcome, then, as a criterion for truth, seems to destroy what the scientist had been thinking of as 'pure research', and to involve control by an outside influence that would determine which things are or are not valuable and worth investigating. It was sufficiently well known to the scientist that most of the greatest scientific discoveries were made by men who had no appreciation or interest in the general utility of the outcome, and whose results were applied only much later and, as it were, by accident. To say, then, that the truth of an idea was influenced by its general value was to run afoul of all the sorely sensitive ideals which the scientist had acquired in his recent contest with the domination of the church. It is hardly to be wondered at, therefore, that the interpretation of pragmatism given by James was not popular with persons of a scientific temperament.

Further, if the value or desirability of an idea has an influence upon its truth, then truth will vary from person to person, for desirability varies with the taste of the person concerned. Peirce had warned against individual standards of truth in his discussion of the Methods of Fixing Belief. The scientific conception, as it had differentiated itself from other conceptions of truth, had attempted to secure a kind of truth not determined by what we would like or by what can be made to seem desirable by oratory or by what can be made to win out over other opinions by skill in debate, but by some criterion quite apart from desire and opinion. Peirce had attempted such a criterion in his postulate of an unchanging eternal reality. Instead, that is, of consulting with each other, of debating with each other to find the truth, we ought to consult this reality. In other words, to undertake scientific experiment. Such had been Peirce's description of the scientific and modern method of attaining truth as contrasted, as he says, with that of the medievalists.

Now the difficulty in Peirce's method, as we have seen, was that this postulate of an external reality unaffected by our opinions would not endure the test for clearness. Every object, says Peirce, reduces to the sum of its effects. The only effect of real things, he says again, is to produce belief. From these two propositions it would seem to follow that reality is a sum of beliefs. But this, of course, eliminates any unchanging reality independent of our opinions about it.

We saw further that Peirce defined both belief and meaning as habit and made no distinction between them. Now as belief and meaning are obviously not the same, we are in need of new definitions for these terms.

At this point we turned to the interpretation of Dewey. For Dewey the distinction would seem to be that while meaning may well be defined as habit, belief is to be defined as expectation. If we believe in anything, this means that we expect certain results from it. To believe is to suppose that if we were to come into relation with the thing we would find certain effects to come about.

From this conception the Deweyan theory of truth would seem to follow immediately. If belief means a sum of expectations, the truth of a belief would mean the verification of these expectations. A true belief simply means one that fulfils expectations.

The Deweyan development of the pragmatic method is obviously very much more in harmony with the procedure of science than that of James. James seems to have 'left the track' in his interpretation of the pragmatic method when he related truth to the predominantly valuable. Truth we have found to have no necessary or invariable connection with general value, for many ideas would be acknowledged to be perfectly true while at the same time being either useless or harmful. For Dewey this matter of value has no place in relation to the test of the truth of an idea, for its truth means nothing more than its ability to lead as it promises.

We seem, then, it may be said in conclusion, to be confronted with something like the following alternatives:

If we believe that Dewey could not have made a correct deduction from the pragmatic method when he developed it into a theory of truth making truth dependent upon fulfilled expectations alone, then very obviously the next step in this investigation is to find the point at which his inference went wrong. This means a re-examination of each step in his reasoning.

If we believe that Dewey does make a correct deduction from the pragmatic method in this development toward truth, then we are confronted with the alternative of either accepting the Deweyan theory of truth or of rejecting the Peircian theory of clearness. That is, if we begin with Peirce on method, we must then go clear through to Dewey on truth. And if we reject Dewey, while believing that Peirce gave a correct description of the method of science, then it seems that we must conclude that the method of science and the method of philosophy are not the same.

Footnotes

1. See for example an article by Alfred Lloyd on "Conformity, Consistency, and Truth" in the Journal of Philosophy for May 22, 1913; also Boodin's Truth and Reality, Caldwell's Pragmatism and Idealism, De Laguna's Dogmatism and Evolution, Murray's Pragmatism, Moore's Pragmatism and Its Critics, and others. Return

2. "The Pragmatic Method", University of California Chronicle 1898. Reprinted in Journal of Philosophy, 1904, v. 1, p. 673. Page references are to the latter. Return

3. "The Meaning of Truth", Preface, p. viii. Return

4. Same, p. 137. Return

5. "The Psychology of Belief", Mind 1889, v. 14, p. 31. Return

6. Vol. II, chapter XXI. Return

7. Mind, N. S. 13, p. 457. Return

8. This paragraph appears as a footnote. Return

9. Boodin: Truth and Reality, pp. 193-4. Return

10. Lee: Vital Lies, vol. 1, pp. 11, 31, 33, 72. Return

11. It is interesting to see that Peirce had the following comment to make in 1878 upon the utility of truth. "Logicality in regard to practical matters is the most useful quality an animal can possess, and might, therefore, result from the action of natural selection; but outside of these it is probably of more advantage to the animal to have his mind filled with pleasing and encouraging visions, independently of their truth; and thus upon impractical subjects, natural selection might occasion a fallacious tendency of thought". (From the first article in the series "Illustrations of the Logic of Science", Popular Science Monthly, vol. 12, p. 3). Return

12. For example, in the Meaning of Truth, pages 195 and 233. Return

13. Mind, N. S. 15, July 1906. Reprinted in "The Influence of Darwin on Philosophy and Other Essays", p. 77. Page references are to the latter. Return

14. What Does Pragmatism Mean by Practical?", Journal of Philosophy, etc., 1908, v. 5, p. 85. Return

15. The last four sentences appear in a footnote. Return

BIBLIOGRAPHY

The Works of Charles Sanders Peirce

1865.	On an improvement of Boole's calculus of logic.	Proc. Am. Acad. Arts and Sci., v. 7, p. 250.
1867.	Logical Papers.	
1868.	Questions concerning certain faculties claimed for man.	Jour. Spec. Phil. 2:103.
	Nominalism and realism.	Jour. Spec. Phil. 2:57.
	On the meaning of 'determined'.	Jour. Spec. Phil. 2:190.
	Some consequences of four incapacities.	Jour. Spec. Phil. 2:140.
	Grounds for the validity of the laws of logic.	Jour. Spec. Phil. 2:193.
1871.	Review and discussion of Fraser's "Works of Berkeley."	No. Am. Rev. 113:449.
1878.	Illustrations of the logic of science.	
	I—The fixation of belief.	Pop. Sci. Mo. 12:1.
	II—How to make our ideas clear.	Pop. Sci. Mo. 12:286.
	III—The doctrine of chances.	Pop. Sci. Mo. 12:604.
	IV—The probability of induction.	Pop. Sci. Mo. 12:705.

1879. Illustrations of the logic of science.

      V—The order of nature.   Pop. Sci. Mo. 13:203.

      VI—Deduction, induction, and hypothesis.   Pop. Sci. Mo. 13:470.

      La logique de la science.   Rev. Philos. 6:553, 7:39.

1880. On the algebra of logic.   Am. Jour. Math. 3:15. Also, Rev. Philos. 12:646.

1883. (Editor) Studies in Logic.

1884. Numerical measure of success of predictions.   Science 4:453.

      Old stone mill at Newport.   Science 4:512.

1888. Logical machines.   Am. Jour. Psy. 1:165.

1890. The architecture of theories.   Monist 1:161.

1891. The doctrine of necessity examined.   Monist 2:321.

      The law of mind.   Monist 2:533.

1892. Man's glassy essence.   Monist 3:1.

      Evolutionary love.   Monist 3:176.

      Reply to the necessitarians.   Monist 3:526.

1896. The regenerated logic.   Monist 7:19.

      The logic of relatives.   Monist 7:161.

1900. Infinitesimals.   Science 11:430.

	Decennial celebration of Clark University.	Science 11:620.
	Century's great men of science.	Smithsonian Institute Reports, 1900, p. 673.
	Annotations on the first three chapters of Pearson's Grammar of Science.	Pop. Sci. Mo. 58:296.
1901.	Campanus.	Science 13:809.
1905.	What pragmatism is.	Monist 15:161.
	The issues of pragmaticism.	Monist 15:481.
1906.	Mr. Peterson's proposed discussion.	Monist 16:147.
	Prolegomena to an apology for pragmaticism.	Monist 16:492.
1908.	Some amazing mazes.	Monist 18:227, 416, 19:36.
	A neglected argument for the reality of God.	Hib. Jour. 7:90.
1910.	On non-Aristotelian logic.	Monist 20:158.

THE WORKS OF WILLIAM JAMES

A "List of the Published Writings of William James" will be found in the Psychological Review for March 1911, v. 18, p. 157.

THE WORKS OF JOHN DEWEY

On Logic and Metaphysics:

1882.	The metaphysical assumptions of	Jour. Spec. Phil.

	materialism.	16:208.
	The pantheism of Spinoza.	Jour. Spec. Phil. 16:249.
1883.	Knowledge and the relativity of feeling.	Jour. Spec. Phil. 17:56.
1884.	Kant and philosophic method.	Jour. Spec. Phil. 18:162.
1886.	The psychological standpoint.	Mind 11:1.
	Psychology as philosophic method.	Mind 11:153.
1887.	"Illusory psychology."	Mind 12:83.
	Knowledge as idealization.	Mind 12:382.
1888.	Leibniz's New Essays Concerning Human Understanding.	
1890.	On some current conceptions of the term 'self'.	Mind 15:58.
1891.	The present position of logical theory.	Monist 2:1.
1892.	The superstition of necessity.	Monist 3:362.
1894.	The ego as cause.	Phil. Rev. 3:337.
1895.	Interest as Related To Will.	
1900.	Some stages of logical thought.	Phil. Rev. 9:465.
1903.	Logical Conditions of a Scientific Treatment of Morality.	
	(And others) Studies in Logical Theory.	
1904.	Notes upon logical topics.	

	I—A classification of contemporary tendencies.	Jour. Phil. 1:57.
	II—The meaning of the term idea.	Jour. Phil. 1:175.
1905.	Immediate empiricism.	Jour. Phil. 2:597.
	The knowledge experience and its relationships.	Jour. Phil. 2:652.
	The knowledge experience again.	Jour. Phil. 2:707.
	The postulate of immediate empiricism.	Jour. Phil. 2:393.
	The realism of pragmatism.	Jour. Phil. 2:324.
1906.	Reality as experience.	Jour. Phil. 3:253.
	The terms 'conscious' and 'consciousness'.	Jour. Phil. 3:39.
	Beliefs and realities.	Phil. Rev. 15:113.
	Experience and objective idealism.	Phil. Rev. 15:465.
	The experimental theory of knowledge.	Mind 15:293.
1907.	The control of ideas by facts.	Jour. Phil. 4:197, 253, 309.
	Pure experience and reality: a disclaimer.	Phil. Rev. 16:419.
	Reality and the criterion for truth of ideas.	Mind 15:317.
1908.	What does pragmatism mean by practical?	Jour. Phil. 5:85.
	Logical character of ideas.	Jour. Phil. 5:375.
1909.	Objects, data, and existence: Reply to Professor McGilvary.	Jour. Phil. 6:13.

	Dilemma of the intellectualistic theory of truth.	Jour. Phil. 6:433.
	Darwin's influence on philosophy.	Pop. Sci. Mo. 75:90.
1910.	Some implications of anti-intellectualism.	Jour. Phil. 7:477.
	Short cuts to realism examined.	Jour. Phil. 7:553.
	Valid knowledge and the subjectivity of experience.	Jour. Phil. 7:169.
	Science as subject-matter and as method.	Science n. s. 31:121.
	How We Think.	
	Influence of Darwin on Philosophy, and Other Essays.	
1911.	Rejoinder to Dr. Spaulding.	Jour. Phil. 8:77.
	Brief studies in realism.	Jour. Phil. 8:393, 546.
	Joint discussion with Dr. Spaulding.	Jour. Phil. 8:574.
1912.	Reply to Professor McGilvary's questions.	Jour. Phil. 9:19.
	In response to Professor McGilvary.	Jour. Phil. 9:544.
	Perception and organic action.	Jour. Phil. 9:645.
	Reply to Professor Royce's critique of instrumentalism.	Phil. Rev. 21:69.

On Psychology, Ethics, Education, etc.:

1890.	Moral theory and practice.	Int. Jour. Ethics 1:186.
1891.	Psychology.	
	Outline of a Critical Theory of Ethics.	
1892.	Green's theory of the moral motive.	Phil. Rev. 1:593.
1893.	Teaching ethics in high school.	Ed. Rev. 6:313.
	Self-realization as the moral ideal.	Phil. Rev. 2:652.
1894.	The psychology of infant language	. Psy. Rev. 1:63.
	The theory of emotion.	
	I—Emotional attitudes.	Psy. Rev. 1:553.
1895.	The theory of emotion.	
	II—The significance of the emotions.	Psy. Rev. 2:13.
1896.	The metaphysical method in ethics.	Psy. Rev. 3:181
	The reflex arc concept in psychology.	Psy. Rev. 3:357.
	Influence of the high school upon educational methods.	Ed. Rev. 4:1.
1897.	The psychology of effort.	Phil. Rev. 6:43.
	(And J. A. McLellan) Psychology of Number and its Application to Methods of Teaching Arithmetic.	
	Evolution and ethics.	Monist 8:321.
	Psychological aspects of school curriculums.	Ed. Rev. 13:356.

1898.	Some remarks on the psychology of number.	Ped. Sem. 5:426.
	W. T. Harris's Psychological Foundation of Education.	Ed. Rev. 16:1.
	Social interpretations.	Phil. Rev. 7:631.
1900.	Psychology and social practice.	Psy. Rev. 7:105.
1901.	Psychology and Social Practice.	
	Are the schools doing what the people want them to do?	Ed. Rev. 21:459.
	The situation as regards the course of study.	Ed. Rev. 22:26.
1902.	The evolutionary method as applied to morality.	
	I—Its scientific necessity.	Phil. Rev. 11:107.
	II—Its significance for conduct.	Phil. Rev. 11:353.
	Interpretation of the savage mind.	Psy. Rev. 9:217.
	Academic freedom.	Ed. Rev. 23:1.
	Problems in secondary education.	Sch. Rev. 19:13.
	Syllabus of courses.	El. Sch. 73:200.
	The school as a social center.	El. Sch. 73:563.
1903.	Emerson: The philosopher of democracy.	Int. Jour. Ethics 13:405.
	Shortening the years of elementary schooling.	Sch. Rev. 11:17.

	The psychological and the logical in teaching geometry.	Ed. Rev. 25:386.
1904.	The philosophical work of Herbert Spencer.	Phil. Rev. 13:159.
1906.	Culture and industry in education.	Ed. Bi-Monthly 1:1.
	The Educational Situation.	
1907.	The life of reason.	Ed. Rev. 34:116.
1908.	(And Tufts) Ethics.	
	Religion and our schools.	Hib. Jour. 6:796.
1909.	Is nature good?	Hib. Jour. 7:827.
	Moral Principles in Education.	
1910.	How We Think.	
	William James.	Jour. Phil. 7:505.
1911.	Is coeducation injurious to girls?	Ladies Home Jour. 28:22.
	Maeterlinck's philosophy of life.	Hib. Jour. 9:765.
1913.	Interest and Effort in Education.	
	An undemocratic proposal.	Vocational Ed. 2:374.
	Industrial education and democracy.	Survey 29:870.

1914.	Report on the Fairhope experiment in organic education.	Survey 32:199.
	National policy of industrial education.	New Republic, v. I.
	Nature and reason in law.	Int. Jour. Eth. 25:25.

Works on Truth

(See also the list under 'Pragmatism').

1624.	Herbert de Clerbury, E.—De Veritate Prout Distinguitur a Revelatione, a Possibiliti et a Falso.
1674.	Malbranche, N.—De la Recherche de la Verite.
1690.	Locke, J.—Essay Concerning the Human Understanding.
1780.	Beattie, James.—An Essay on the Nature and Immutability of Truth.
1781.	Kant, Im.—Kritik der reinen Vernunft.
1800.	Kant, Im.—Logik.
1811.	Fries, J.—System der Logik, p. 448 ff.
1817.	Hegel, F.—Encyclopädie. Sec. 21.
1826.	Hume, D.—Treatise on Human Nature. iv, sec. 2.
1840.	Abercombie, J.—An Inquiry Concerning

the Intellectual Powers and the Investigation of Truth.

1842. Thomson, W.—Outlines of the Necessary Laws of Thought.

1854. Bailey, S.—Essays on the Pursuit of Truth.

1862. Tiberghien, G.—Logique. v. 2, pp. 322-355.

1866. Hamilton, Sir Wm.—Logic. Lectures 28-31.

1875. Forster, W.—Wahrheit und Wahrschleinlichkeit.

1877. Jevons, W. S.—The Principles of Science. 2nd ed., pp. 374-396.

1878. Schuppe, W.—Logik. v. 1, pp. 622-696.

1880. Wundt, W.—Logik.

1882. Bergmann, J.—Die Grundprobleme der Logik. p. 96ff.

1884. Schulbert-Soldern, R. von.—Grundlagen einer Erkenntnisstheorie. p. 156ff.

1885. Royce, J.—The Religious Aspect of Philosophy.

1889. Argyle, Duke of—What Is Truth?

Stephen, L.—On some kinds of necessary truth. Mind 14:50, 188.

1890. Carus, Paul—The criterion of truth. Monist 1:229.

1892. Rickert, H.—Der Gegenstand der

Erkenntniss. Freib. pp. 63-64.

1893. Bradley, F. H.—Appearance and Reality. Chapters 16, 24.

Cousin, Victor—Lectures on the True, the Beautiful, and the Good.

Soyen, Shakn—Universality of truth. Monist 4:161.

Miller, D. S.—The meaning of truth and error. Phil. Rev. 2:408.

Smith, W.—Certitude. Phil. Rev. 2:665.

1894. Gordy, J. P.—The test of belief. Phil. Rev. 3:257.

1895. Jerusalem, W.—Die Urteilsfunction. p. 185ff.

Bosanquet, B.—Essentials of Logic. pp. 69-79.

Sigwart, C.—Logic. v. 1, pp. 295-326.

1896. Hodder, A.—Truth and the tests of truth. Phil. Rev. 5:1.

Wundt, W.—Ueber naiven und kritischen Realismus. Phil. Studien 12:332.

1897. Brochard, Victor—De L'Erreur.

Jordan, D. S.—The stability of truth. Pop. Sci. Mo. 4:642, 749.

Strümpell, Ludw.—Unterchiede der Wahrheiten und irrtümer. p. 58.

1898. Baillie, J. B.—Truth and history. Mind 7:506.

Powell, J. W.—Truth and Error.

1899.	Eisler, W.—Wörterbuch der philosophischen Begriffe.	
1900.	Sidgwick, H.—Criteria of truth and error.	Mind 9:8.
1901.	Creighton, J. E.—Methodology and truth.	Phil. Rev. 10:408.
	French, F. C.—The doctrine of the twofold truth.	Phil. Rev. 10:477.
	Royce, J.—The World and the Individual.	
	Smyth, J.—Truth and Reality.	
1902.	Baldwin, J. M.—Development and Evolution. Chapter 17.	
	Pritchett, H. S.—What is truth?	Outlook 70:620.
1903.	Duprat, Guillaume L.—Le Mesonge. Etude de psycho-sociologie pathologique et normale.	
	Pilate's What is truth.	Catholic World 77:705.
1904.	Bradley, F. H.—On truth and practice.	Mind 13:309.
	Glasenapp, G. v.—Der Wert der Wahrheit.	Zeitsch. f. Philos. u. phil. Kr. 123:186, 124:25.
	Rogers, A. K.—James on humanism and truth.	Jour. Phil. 1:693.
1905.	Alexander, H. B.—Phenomenalism and the problem of knowledge.	Jour. Phil. 2:182.
	Alexander, H. B.—Quantity, quality, and the function of knowledge.	Jour. Phil. 2:459.

	Hyslop, J. H.—Problems of Philosophy. Chapter 7.	
	Joachim, H. H.—'Absolute' and 'relative' truth.	Mind 14:1.
	Joseph, H. W. B.—Professor James on 'humanism and truth'.	Mind 14:28.
	Knox, H. V.—Mr. Bradley's absolute criterion.	Mind 14:210.
	Overstreet, H. A.—Conceptual completeness and abstract truth.	Phil. Rev. 14:308.
	Pitkin, W. B.—Psychology of eternal truths.	Jour. Phil. 2:449.
	Taylor, A. E.—Truth and practice.	Phil. Rev. 14:265.
1906.	Gore, George—Scientific sketch of untruth.	Monist 16:96.
	Russell, B.—The nature of truth.	Mind 15:528.
	Review of Joachim's The Nature of Truth.	Nation 83:42.
	Schiller, F. C. S.—The ambiguity of truth.	Mind 15:161.
	Schiller, F. C. S.—Joachim's The Nature of Truth.	Jour. Phil. 3:549.
	Taylor, A. E.—Truth and consequences.	Mind 15:81.
	Openmindedness.	Catholic World 82:756.
1908.	Bakewell, C. M.—On the meaning of truth.	Phil. Rev. 17:579.
	Creighton, J. E.—The nature and criterion of truth.	Phil. Rev. 17:592.

	Gardiner, H. N.—The problems of truth.	Phil. Rev. 17:113.
	Moore, A. W.—Truth value.	Jour. Phil. 5:429.
	Prat, J. B.—Truth and ideas.	Jour. Phil. 5:122.
	Urbana, F. M.—On a supposed criterion of the absolute truth of some propositions.	Jour. Phil. 5:701.
1909.	Bradley, F. H.—On truth and coherence.	Mind 18:322.
	Bradley, F. H.—Coherence and contradiction.	Mind 18:489.
	Buckham, J. W.—Organization of truth.	Int. Jour. Eth. 20:63.
	Carritt, E. F.—Truth in art and religion.	Hib. Jour. 8:362.
	Knox, H. V.—The evolution of truth.	Quarterly Rev. No. 419.
1910.	Alexander, H. B.—Truth and nature.	Monist 20:585.
	Boodin, J. E.—The nature of truth.	Phil. Rev. 19:395.
	Bradley, F. H.—On appearance, error, and contradiction.	Mind 19:153.
	Jacobson, Edmund—Relational account of truth.	Jour. Phil. 7:253.
	Russell, B.—Philosophical Essays.	Essays 5, 6, 7.
	Schmidt, Karl—Hertz's theory of truth.	Monist 20:445.
	Tsanoff, R. A.—Professor Boodin on the nature of truth.	Phil. Rev. 19:632.
	Plea for the half-truth.	Atlantic 105:576.
	Truth as once for all delivered.	Bib. World 35:219.

1911.	Alexander, H. B.—Goodness and beauty of truth.	Jour. Phil. 5:29.
	Boodin, J. E.—The divine five-fold truth.	Monist 21:288.
	Boodin, J. E.—The nature of truth: a reply.	Phil. Rev. 20:59.
	Boodin, J. E.—Truth and Reality.	
	Bradley, F. F.—On some aspects of truth.	Mind 20:305.
	Carus, Paul—Truth on Trial.	
	McGilvary, E. B.—The 'fringe' of William James's psychology as the basis of logic.	Phil. Rev. 20:137.
	Rother, A. J.—Certitude.	
	Royce, J.—William James, and Other Essays.	
	Self-sufficiency of truth.	Bib. World 37:147.
1912.	Fawcett, E. D.—Truth's 'original object'.	Mind 21:89.
	Larson, C. D.—What Is Truth?	
	Leuba, J. H.—Religion and the discovery of truth.	Jour. Phil. 9:406.
	Review of Jordan's Stability of Truth.	Int. Jour. Eth. 23:92.
	Zahlfeisch, Johann—Ist die Lüge erlaubt?	Archiv. f. system. Philos. 18:241.
1913.	Alexander, S.—Collective willing and truth.	Mind 22:14, 161.
	Gerould, K. F.—Boundarie of truth.	Atlantic 112:454.
	Lloyd, A. H.—Conformity, consistency, and truth.	Jour. Phil. 10:281.

	Moore, A. W.—The aviary theory of truth and error.	Jour. Phil. 10:542.
	Wright, W. K.—Genesis of the categories.	Jour. Phil. 10:645.
	Wright, H. W.—Practical success as the criterion of truth.	Phil. Rev. 22:606.
1914.	Bowman, A. A.—The problem of knowledge from the standpoint of validity.	Phil. Rev. 23:1, 146, 299.
	Bradley, F. H.—Essays on Truth and Reality.	
	Broad, C. D.—Mr. Bradley on truth and reality.	Mind 23:349.
	Capron, F. H.—Anatomy of Truth.	
	Leighton, J. A.—Truth, reality, and relation.	Phil. Rev. 23:17.
	Rother, A. J.—Truth and Error.	
	Sidgwick, A.—Truth and working.	Mind 23:99.
	Strange, E. H.—Objectives, truth, and error.	Mind 23:489.

Works on Pragmatism

(See also the list under 'Truth').

1900.	Caldwell, W.—Pragmatism.	Mind 9:433.
1902.	Schiller, F. C. S.—'Useless' knowledge.	Mind 11:196.
	Schiller, F. C. S.—Axioms As Postulates.	

1903. King, Irving—Pragmatism as a philosophical method. — Phil. Rev. 12:511.

Schiller, F. C. S.—Humanism: Philosophical Essays.

1904. Bawden, Heath—What is pragmatism? — Jour. Phil. 1:421.

Creighton, J. E.—Purpose as a logical category. — Phil. Rev. 13:284.

Leighton, J. A.—Pragmatism. — Jour. Phil. 1:148.

1905. Bode, B. H.—Pure experience and the external world. — Jour. Phil. 2:128.

Bode, B. H.—The cognitive experience and its object. — Jour. Phil. 2:658.

Bode, B. H.—The concept of pure experience. — Phil. Rev. 14:684.

Hoernle, R. F. A.—Pragmatism versus absolutism. — Mind 14:297, 441.

King, Irving—Pragmatic interpretation of the Christian dogma. — Monist 15:248.

Moore, A. W.—Pragmatism and its critics. — Phil. Rev. 14:284.

Schiller, F. C. S.—The definition of 'pragmatism' and 'humanism'. — Mind 14:235.

1906. Bode, B. H.—Realism and pragmatism. — Jour. Phil. 3:393.

Colvin, S. S.—Pragmatism, old and new. — Monist 16:547.

	Rogers, A. K.—Professor James' theory of knowledge.	Phil. Rev. 15:577.
	Rousmaniere, F. H.—A definition of experimentation.	Jour. Phil. 3:673.
	Russell, J. E.—Pragmatism's meaning of truth.	Jour. Phil. 3:599.
	Russell, J. E.—Some difficulties with the epistemology of pragmatism and radical empiricism.	Phil. Rev. 15:406.
	Schiller, F. C. S.—Pragmatism and pseudo-pragmatism.	
	Sturt, H.—Idola Theatri, a Criticism of Oxford Thought and Thinkers from the Standpoint of Personal Idealism.	Mind 15:375.
	Vailati, Giovanni—Pragmatism and mathematical logic.	Monist 16:481.
1907.	Brown, W. A.—Pragmatic value of the absolute.	Jour. Phil. 4:459.
	Bush, W. T.—Papini on Introduzione al prafmatismo.	Jour. Phil. 4:639.
	Foster, G. B.—Pragmatism and knowledge.	Am. Jour. Theol. 11:591.
	Moore, A. W.—Perry on pragmatism.	Jour. Phil. 4:567.
	Nichols, H.—Pragmatism versus science.	Jour. Phil. 4:122.
	Papini, G.—What pragmatism is like.	Pop. Sci. Mo. 71:351.

Perry, R. B.—A review of pragmatism as a philosophical generalization.	Jour. Phil. 4:421.
Perry, R. B.—A review of pragmatism as a theory of knowledge.	Jour. Phil. 4:365.
Pratt, J. B.—Truth and its verification.	Jour. Phil. 4:320.
Review of Schiller's Humanism.	Nation 84:436.
Review of Papini's Tragico Quotidiano.	Nation 85:521.
Reviews of James's Pragmatism.	Bookman 26:215. No. Am. 185:884. Science n. s. 26:464. Nation 85:57. Ind. 63:630.
Schiller, F. C. S.—The pragmatic babe in the woods.	Jour. Phil. 4:42.
Schiller, F. C. S.—Cure of doubt.	Jour. Phil. 4:235.
Schiller, F. C. S.—Pragmatism versus skepticism.	Jour. Phil. 4:482.
Schiller, F. C. S.—Studies in Humanism.	
Schiller, F. C. S.—Review of James's Pragmatism.	Mind 16:593.
Sellars, R. W.—Dewey's view of agreement.	Jour. Phil. 4:432.
Shorey, P.—Equivocation of pragmatism.	Dial 43:273.

	Slosson, E. E.—What is pragmatism?	Ind. 62:422.
	Talbot, Ellen B.—The philosophy of Fichte in its relation to pragmatism.	Phil. Rev. 16:488.
	Fascination of the pragmatic method.	Cur. Lit. 43:186.
	A new philosophy.	Harper's W. 51:1264.
	The newest philosophy.	Cur. Lit. 42:652.
	Pragmatic philosophy.	Ind. 62:797.
	Pragmatism, a new philosophy.	Ed. Rev. 34:227.
	Where pragmatism fails.	Cur. Lit. 46:415.
1908.	Armstrong, A. C.—Evolution of pragmatism.	Jour. Phil. 5:645.
	Bawden, H. H.—New philosophy called pragmatism.	Pop. Sci. Mo. 73:61.
	Bradley, F. H.—On the ambiguity of pragmatism.	Mind 17:226.
	Burke, J. B.—Fashionable philosophy at Oxford and Harvard.	Liv. Age 257:559.
	Bush, W. T.—Provisional and eternal truth.	Jour. Phil. 5:181.
	Carus, Paul—Pragmatism.	Monist 18:321.
	Hebert, M.—Le Pragmatisme. Etude de ses Diverse Formes.	
	Hibben, J. B.—The test of pragmatism.	Phil. Rev. 17:365.

	Lovejoy, A. O.—Thirteen pragmatisms.	Jour. Phil. 5:5, 29.
	Lovejoy, A. O.—Pragmatism and theology.	Am. Jour. Theol. 12:116.
	McGilvary, E. B.—British exponents of pragmatism.	Hib. Jour. 6:632.
	McTaggart, J. E.—Review of James's Pragmatism.	Mind 17:104.
	Salter, W. M.—A. new philosophy.	Atlantic 101:657.
	Schiller, F. C. S.—Is Mr. Bradley a pragmatism?	Mind 17:370.
	Schiller, F. C. S.—British exponents of pragmatism.	Hib. Jour. 6:903.
	Schinz, A.—Dewey's pragmatism.	Jour. Phil. 5:617.
	Sidgwick, A.—The ambiguity of pragmatism.	Mind 17:368.
	Strong, A. L.—Religious aspects of pragmatism.	Am. Jour. Theol. 12:231.
	Strong, C. A.—Pragmatism and its definition of truth.	Jour. Phil. 5:256.
	Vialiti, G.—A pragmatic zoologist.	Monist 18:142.
1909.	Agnew, P. G.—What is pragmatism?	Forum 41:70.
	Carus, Paul—A German critic of pragmatism.	Monist 19:136.
	Carus, Paul—A postscript on pragmatism.	Monist 19:85.
	Carus, Paul—Professor John Hibben on 'the	Monist 19:319.

test of pragmatism'.

Corrance, H. C.—Review of Hebert's Le Pragmatisme.	Hib. Jour. 7:218.
Cox, J. W.—Concepts of truth and reality.	Am. Cath. Q. 34:139.
Huizinga, A. V.—The American philosophy pragmatism.	Bib. Sac. 66:78.
Kallen, H. M.—Affiliations of pragmatism.	Jour. Phil. 6:655.
Kallen, H. M.—Dr. Montague and the pragmatic notion of value.	Jour. Phil. 6:549.
Knox, H. V.—Pragmatism: the evolution of truth.	Quarterly Rev. 210:379.
Ladd, G. T.—The confusion of pragmatism.	Hib. Jour. 7:784.
McGilvary, E. B.—British exponents of pragmatism (A rejoinder).	Hib. Jour. 7:443.
Montague, W. P.—The true, the good, and the beautiful from a pragmatic standpoint.	Jour. Phil. 6:233.
Montague, W. P.—May a realist be a pragmatist?	Jour. Phil. 6:460, 485, 543, 501.
Moore, A. W.—"Anti-pragmatisme."	Jour. Phil. 6:291.
Moore, T. V.—Pragmatism of William James.	Catholic World 90:341.
Moore, A. W.—Pragmatism and solipsism.	Jour. Phil. 6:378.

More, P. E.—New stage of pragmatism.	Nation 88:456.
Murray, D. L.—Pragmatic realism.	Mind 18:377.
Pratt, J. B.—What Is Pragmatism?	
Pratt, J. B.—What is pragmatism?	Am. Jour. Theol. 13:477.
Schiller, F. C S.—Humanism and intuition.	Mind 18:125.
Schiller, F. C. S.—Logic as psychology.	Mind 18:400.
Schiller, F. C. S.—Humanism, intuitionism, and objective reality.	Mind 18:570.
Schinz, A.—Anti-pragmatisme.	
Schinz, A.—Rousseau a forerunner of pragmatism.	Monist 19:481.
Schinz, A.—A few words in reply to Professor Moore's criticism of 'Anti-pragmatism'.	Jour. Phil. 6:434.
Shackleford, T. M.—What pragmatism is, as I understand it.	Pop. Sci. Mo. 75:571.
Taylor, A. E.—Review of James's Pluralistic Universe.	Mind 18:576.
Tausch, Edwin—William James the pragmatist.	Monist 19:1.
Origin of pragmatism.	Nation 88:358.
Philosophy in the open.	Bookman 29:661.
Pragmatism as a strangler of literature.	Cur. Lit. 46:637.

1910. Boodin, J. E.—Pragmatic realism.   Monist 20:602.

Carus, Paul—Pragmatist view of truth.   Monist 20:139.

Carus, Paul—Truth.   Monist 20:481.

Cockrell, T. D. A.—Is pragmatism pragmatic?   Dial 48:422.

De Laguna, T.—Dogmatism and Evolution.

Fite, W.—O'Sullivan's Old Criticism and New Pragmatism.   Jour. Phil. 7:499.

Gillespie, C. M.—The truth of Protagoras.   Mind 19:470.

Jacoby, Gunther—Der Pragmatismus.

Kallen, H. M.—James, Bergson, and Mr. Pitkin.   Jour. Phil. 7:353.

Lee, V.—Two pragmatisms.   No. Am. 192:449.

Lloyd, A. H.—Possible idealism of a pluralist.   Am. Jour. Theol. 14:406.

Macintosh, D. C.—Pragmatic element in the teaching of Paul.   Am. Jour. Theol. 13:361.

McGiffert, A. C.—The pragmatism of Kant.   Jour. Phil. 7:197.

Miller, D. S.—Some of the tendencies of Professor James's work.   Jour. Phil. 7:645.

Moore, A. W.—Pragmatism and Its Critics.

Moore, A. W.—How ideas work.   Jour. Phil. 7:617.

O'Sullivan, J. M.—Old Criticism and New Pragmatism.

Russell, B.—Philosophical Essays. Chapters 4, 6.

Reviews of James's Meaning of Truth. Nation 90:88. Hib. Jour. 8:904. Ed. Rev. 40:201.

Russell, J. E.—Review of James's Meaning of Truth. Jour. Phil. 7:22.

Schinz, A.—Anti-pragmatism.

Shackelford, T. M.—What is pragmatism? Sci. Am. S. 70:78.

Sidgwick, A.—The Application of Logic.

Stettheimer, E.—Rowland's Right To Believe. Jour. Phil. 7:330.

Walker, L. J.—Theory of Knowledge: Absolutism, Pragmatism, and Realism.

1911. Brown, H. C.—De Laguna's Dogmatism and Evolution. Jour. Phil. 8:556.

Cockerell, T. D. A.—Reality and truth. Pop. Sci. Mo. 78:371.

Eastman, Max—Dewey's How We Think. Jour. Phil. 8:244.

Fawcett, E. D.—A note on pragmatism. Mind 20:399.

Jacks, L. P.—William James and his message. Contemp. Rev. 99:20.

	Kallen, H. M.—Boutroux's William James.	Jour. Phil. 8:583.
	Kallen, H. M.—Pragmatism and its 'principles'.	Jour. Phil. 8:617.
	More, P. E.—The Pragmatism of William James.	
	Patten, S. N.—Pragmatism and social science.	Jour. Phil. 8:653.
	Pratt, J. B.—The religious philosophy of William James.	Hib. Jour. 10:225.
	Riley, I. W.—Continental critics of pragmatism.	Jour. Phil. 8:225, 289.
	Russell, J. E.—Truth as value and the value of truth.	Mind 20:538.
	Schiller, F. C. S.—Article 'pragmatism' in Encyclopedia Brittanica.	
	Schiller, F. C. S.—Review of James's Some Problems of Philosophy.	Mind 20:571.
	Turner, W.—Pragmatism: what does it mean?	Cath. World 94:178.
	Vibbert, C. B.—Moore's Pragmatism and its Critics.	Jour. Phil. 8:468.
1912.	Berkeley, H.—The kernel of pragmatism.	Mind 21:84.
	Ceulemans, J. B.—Metaphysics of pragmatism.	Am. Cath. Q. 37:310.
	Jacoby, Gunther—Bergson, pragmatism, and Schopenhauer.	Monist 22:593.

Kallen, H. M.—Royce's William James.	Jour. Phil. 9:548.
Lee, Vernon—Vital Lies. v. 1, part 1.	
Lee, Vernon—What is truth? a criticism of pragmatism.	Yale Rev. n. s. 1:600.
Loewenberg, J.—Vaihinger's Die Philosophie des Als	Ob. Jour. Phil. 9:717.
Macintosh, D. C.—Representational pragmatism.	Mind 21:167.
Montague, W. P.—Review of James's Some Problems of Philosophy.	Jour. Phil. 9:22.
Murray, D. L.—Pragmatism.	
Reviews of Moore's Pragmatism and Its Critics.	Nation 92:13. Int Jour. Eth. 22:222.
Riley, I. W.—Huizinga's The American Philosophy Pragmatism.	Jour. Phil. 9:248.
Russell, B.—Review of James's Essays in Radical Empiricism.	Mind 21:571.
Russell, J. E.—Bergson's anti-intellectualism.	Jour. Phil. 9:129.
Schiller, F. C. S.—Formal Logic, A Scientific and Social Problem.	
Schiller, F. C. S.—The 'working' of 'truth'.	Mind 21:532.

1913.
Alexander, S.—Collective willing and truth.	Mind 22:14, 161.
Boodin, J. E.—Pragmatic realism.—The five	Mind 22:509.

attributes.

Carr, H. W.—Logic and life.	Mind 22:484.
Carr, H. W.—The Problem of Truth.	
Caldwell, W.—Pragmatism and Idealism.	
Knox, H. V.—William James and his philosophy.	Mind 22:231.
Moore, A. W.—Pragmatism, science, and truth.	
Perry, R. B.—Realism and pragmatism.	Mind 22:544.
Review of Vernon Lee's Vital Lies.	Nation 96:414.
Royce, J.—Psychological problems emphasized by pragmatism.	Pop. Sci. Mo. 83:394.
Schiller, F. C. S.—The 'working' of truths and their 'criterion'.	Mind 22:532.
Schiller, F. C. S.—Humanism.	
Stebbing, L. S.—The 'working' of 'truths'.	Mind 22:250.
Wright, W. K.—Practical success as the criterion of truth.	Phil. Rev. 22:606.

1914. Knox, H. V.—Philosophy of William James.

Moore, J. S.—Value in its relation to meaning and purpose.	Jour. Phil. 11:184.
Ross, G. R. T.—Aristotle and abstract truth—A reply to Mr. Schiller.	Mind 23:396.
Sidgwick, A.—Truth and working.	Mind 23:99.

Stebbing, L. S.—Pragmatism and French Voluntarism.

Wilde, N.—The pragmatism of Pascal.   Phil. Rev. 23:540.

Can socialism be identified with pragmatism?   Cur. Opinion 56:45.

VITA.

The writer was born in 1884 at Pomeroy, Ohio, and received his earlier education in the country schools near that city. His college preparatory work was done in the high school of Roswell, New Mexico, from which he was graduated in 1906. He then entered immediately the University of Wisconsin, and from this institution received the Bachelor's degree in 1910 and the Master's degree in 1911. From 1911 to 1914, while acting as fellow or as assistant, he studied in the graduate school of the University of Illinois.

Milton Keynes UK
Ingram Content Group UK Ltd.
UKHW050241220624
444555UK00005BA/474